Introducing Pattern Cutting

Introducing Pattern Cutting

Ann Tuit

Heinemann Educational Books · London

Heinemann Educational Books Ltd
London Edinburgh Melbourne Auckland Toronto
Singapore Hong Kong Kuala Lumpur
Ibadan Nairobi Johannesburg
Lusaka New Delhi Kingston

ISBN 0 435 42860 8

© Ann Tuit 1974
First published 1974
Reprinted 1975, 1976, 1978

Published by Heinemann Educational Books Ltd
48 Charles Street, London W1X 8AH
Printed in Great Britain by Biddles Ltd, Guildford, Surrey

Contents

Introduction

Although there are many pattern cutting books already on the market, most are very difficult for a beginner to follow without guidance from a teacher. This book is intended to help the complete beginner in pattern cutting—the 'A' level needlework student, the first year college student, and the keen and experienced amateur dressmaker who wishes to progress to making her own patterns. The book is designed to explain and illustrate the principles underlying pattern cutting, not simply as a reference book from which complete dress styles may be copied.

Successful pattern cutting depends on analyzing the design into its component parts and adapting each part step-by-step until the pattern is complete. In line with this, most of the illustrations show how to cut only one area of the pattern and several adaptations must be combined to produce the complete pattern. The examples have been chosen to demonstrate the principles of pattern cutting in the simplest possible way and once these principles have been thoroughly understood, the student will be able to devise a method of cutting any style.

It is most important, however, that the pattern cutter should not copy the diagrams line for line, but should preserve a sense of originality and make use of fashion sense combined with a knowledge of the most flattering line and shape for her own figure type.

Explanation of Terms Used

Blocks

Blocks are the 5 pieces which are outlined and adapted to make a pattern: front bodice, back bodice, sleeve, front skirt and back skirt (also front and back trouser blocks). Blocks may be made in paper or card but are more useful if constructed in card. The blocks themselves are never cut or used for cutting fabric, but are outlined on to paper and adapted to the style required—by moving the darts to other positions, adding extra seams or fullness, adding collars, cuffs, etc.

Pattern

The pattern is made when the blocks are outlined and adapted to the required style, as explained above. Therefore, the five blocks always remain the same shapes but the shapes of the pattern pieces vary according to the style for which the pattern is being cut.

It is important to be quite clear about the difference between blocks and patterns.

Square out or square across

Draw a line at right angles to the line previously mentioned.

Fold out (a dart)

Fold the pattern along one edge of the dart and place it to the other edge so that the dart no longer exists. Half of the dart may also be folded out by placing the folded edge to the centre point of the dart.

Balance points

Balance points are marked on two corresponding parts of a pattern to show exactly how the parts should be joined together (see page 12).

Abbreviations

m/ment	measurement
a/h	armhole
s/h	sleevehead
c/f	centre front
c/b	centre back
u/arm	under arm

Scale

All diagrams are drawn to ¼ scale, with the exception of the capes, which are drawn to $\frac{1}{8}$ scale.

Blocks

The type of pattern cutting which is used here is known as 'flat' pattern cutting or 'pattern drafting'. It is a method of obtaining patterns by working from the m/ments of the figure according to a set of instructions and drawing a shape on paper or card. The alternative is to work directly on a dress stand, either using a cheap fabric such as calico or muslin which is then used as a pattern to cut the fabric, or using the fabric itself. This system is known as 'modelling' and although it is the only suitable method for draped styles (as it enables the exact position and amount of fullness to be controlled), it would be very expensive and time-consuming to make every pattern by modelling.

There are two stages in pattern drafting: the making of a set of five basic patterns known as 'block patterns' or 'blocks', and secondly the adaptation of the blocks to the style required. The five blocks are—front and back bodice, sleeve and front and back skirt. The advantage of cutting from blocks is that the blocks provide a permanent record of the correct fit while dart movements, additional seams, fullness, etc., are planned on them. Cutting from blocks has the added advantage of being quicker than any other system. The method of using the same set of blocks to adapt to any style shows that all styles, no matter how different they may appear, must be related since they are all developed from the same basic shape and will thus fit the same figure.

It therefore follows that unless the fit of the blocks is perfect, no pattern cut from them will fit well, and it is worth spending time on making up your set of blocks in calico to check the fit. Any adjustments needed must first be made in the fabric and then transferred to the blocks. From then on, the cutter may have complete confidence in adapting the revised blocks to any style, knowing that any pattern developed from the blocks will have the same good fit.

Having checked the fit of the blocks, it is advisable to make a set of blocks in cardboard as they may then be outlined quickly and will be better able to stand up to frequent use. Plastic coated card is preferable as it does not wear at the edges. Blocks are always made without seam allowances as they are then very much easier to adapt and the seam allowances may be added to the final pattern, if required. All the patterns shown in the diagrams are without seam allowances for the sake of simplicity.

The block instructions which follow have been developed from my own experience and I have found them to be an extremely good fit and also simple to draft due to the logical sequence of work. The construction lines, which are drawn first, help to show the relation between the block and the figure, which is very important. It is therefore essential that the construction lines (bust line, front and back width lines, hip line, etc) are transferred when the block is outlined to make a pattern.

The back bodice block has two darts—one at the waist and one at the shoulder (to provide room for the shoulder blades). The front bodice block has only one dart, at the waist. Many blocks have a shoulder dart instead, or a shoulder and a waist dart, but the single waist dart most clearly illustrates the reason why a dart is needed in the front bodice, i.e. because the dart is formed of the difference between the bust and waist m/ments. This difference is known as the 'waist suppression'. It also clearly shows that the greater the difference, the wider the dart needs to be.

The waist suppression must be distributed around the figure to avoid creasing caused by over-shaping in one area and a loose fit in another area. The side seam can only take a small amount of suppression before it begins to crease but a further amount may be taken at the back, below the shoulder blades, thus the back block has a dart in that position. However it is obvious that, for the female figure, most of the suppression needs to be at the front, hence the large dart in the front bodice block.

The reason underlying the shape of the bodice blocks can further be demonstrated by making a plain bodice by modelling fabric directly on a dress stand. It will be found that the fabric cannot be fitted over the front of the stand without fullness appearing somewhere around the edge of the fabric. If it is first pinned along the c/f and over the shoulder area, and then smoothed along the u/arm seam, the fullness will be concentrated at the waist and will fall under the bust point. This is the position in which it is shown on the block. Pinning a piece of fabric over the back of the stand will produce similar results, with the fullness concentrated beneath the shoulder blades. This shows that the results produced by an accurate system of pattern drafting are identical to those produced by modelling.

The sleeve block is completely straight at the sides and this shape was chosen because it is much easier to adapt than a block which tapers at the sides.

The skirt blocks are very slightly flared at the sides, but this is the minimum recommended hem width since a skirt which is completely straight at the sides will appear to taper inwards.

Blocks are not intended to be used as patterns, i.e. for cutting out fabric, without being adapted and are not suitable for use without adaptation for several reasons. For instance, the front dart on the bodice block extends to the bust point (to ensure that a dart drawn in any position [see pages 24-27] will always point towards the bust point) but the bust darts on a pattern must always be shortened 1"-2" (2.5cm-5.0cm). Also the dart in the front bodice block is very wide since it contains most of the waist suppression, but it would not be practical to make a dress with such a large dart as it would badly distort the grain of the fabric. Two smaller darts give a much better fit when a tightly fitted bodice is required. See bodice section—page 24 onwards.

Drafting the Blocks

All bust, waist and hip m/ments referred to are 'net', i.e. without ease. All horizontal construction lines *must* be parallel to each other and at right angles to all vertical lines.

Bodice and skirt blocks are always drafted with the c/b on the left hand side and the c/f on the right hand side, and similarly the sleeve is drafted with the back on the left hand side of the centre line and the front on the right hand side. The complete set of blocks therefore fits the right hand side of the figure. The only reason is that the majority of blocks are set out in this way and it is therefore easier to understand other blocks and to compare them. All commercial patterns are arranged in this way as are most pattern cutting books, although the blocks in some American books may be reversed.

All the curves which are drawn during the drafting of the blocks should be regarded as provisional and must be corrected after the blocks have been completed by placing corresponding edges together and checking that the curves are smooth and continuous across the seams. For instance, on the bodice blocks, place the shoulder seams together to check the curves of neckline and a/h, place the side seams together to check the curves of a/h and waist. On the skirt blocks place the side seams together, first at the waist to check the curve of the waistline, then at the hem to check the hemline curve. Place the sleeve seams together to check the curves of s/h and wrist.

Since the blocks represent only half of the front or back, all lines which join to the c/f or c/b must join at right angles to ensure that the line is continuous when the complete section is opened out. Diag 1 shows a badly shaped neckline resulting in a point at the c/f. The broken line shows the correct shape. The a/h has also been badly shaped resulting in a point at the shoulder instead of a continuous curve. The broken line shows the correct line.

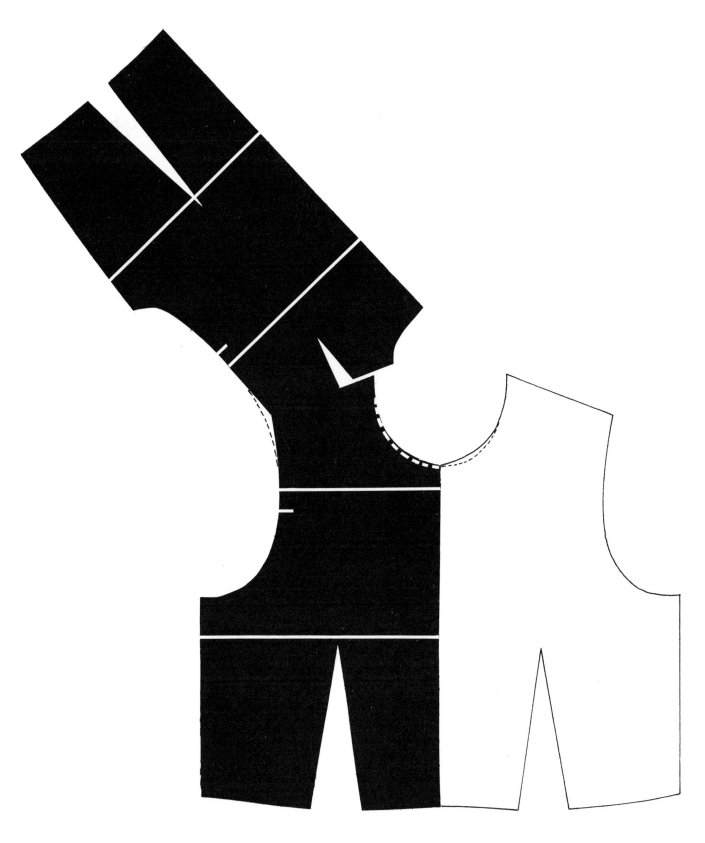

Before drafting blocks to your own m/ments, practise drafting them in stock sizes so that the shape and proportions may be compared with the diags (on pages 11—17). This provides a valuable lesson in the appreciation of line and proportion, which is so important in good pattern cutting. Also practise drawing smoothly curved lines as it is vital that the curved lines on a pattern are drawn smoothly with gradual, never abrupt, changes of direction, and that curves are joined very smoothly into straight lines. Patterns may be drafted using tailor's chalk instead of pencil and many people find it easier to draw a good line with the edge of a piece of chalk. There is no need to try to memorize the draft of the blocks as it will be memorized naturally with practice.

Taking Measurements

It is essential that measurements are taken accurately; that is, in the correct positions and with an equal amount of tension on the tape, as inaccurate m/ments will cause an unnecessary amount of fitting and re-cutting after the garment is tacked together. There are two reasons for taking m/ments: to ascertain the size of the figure, and to determine the proportions of the various parts of the figure. Skill in taking m/ments accurately will be attained with practice and it may be found helpful to practise on a dress stand to gain confidence in correct positioning of the tape.

Make a general observation of the shape of the figure before taking m/ments and note any variations from normal, such as unusually sloping or square shoulders, and note the posture of the figure, whether normal, erect or stooping. Study the side view in addition to the front and back views as this gives a better indication of the posture and proportion.

Before beginning to take m/ments, tie a piece of tape around the waist of the figure to define the exact location of the waist, so that accurate m/ments may be taken to and from the tape. (This is very important as it is otherwise difficult to assess the position of the waist accurately, especially at the back.)

Measurements may be taken over a dress if it is close fitting, or over underclothes. Always take m/ments in the same order each time to avoid omitting any, and do not allow ease when measuring as this is allowed later when drafting the pattern. The numbers refer to the sketch on page 7, and to the measurement chart on page 9.

Dress

1 Bust
This m/ment is usually taken first as it gives an indication of the other m/ments to expect if the figure is in proportion. The tape should be slightly raised at the back to cover the shoulder blades. This is important as, if the tape is allowed to slip down, the m/ment may be too small by 1" or 2" (2.5cm to 5.0cm).

2 High bust
If the bust of the figure is prominent in relation to the remainder of the figure, it is advisable to take a high bust m/ment above the usual bust m/ment just under the arms. This m/ment should be checked against the m/ment of the bodice blocks along the u/arm lines.

3 Waist
Always take this m/ment even if it is not absolutely necessary, (as in the case of loose fitting clothes) as it gives an indication of the proportions of the figure. Measure closely but not tightly.

4 Hip
This m/ment is taken over the widest part of the hips which may be anywhere between 7" and 11" (17.8cm-27.9cm) below the waist, but is usually 8"-9" (20.3cm-22.9cm) below. Always stand at the side of the figure when taking the hip m/ment as the correct level for the tape can then be clearly seen. Most people tend to take this m/ment too high. When the hip m/ment is found to be large in relation to the bust and waist, note the position of the excess—whether at the back (large seat) or at the side (prominent hips).

5 Hip depth
The distance between the waist and the level at which the hip is measured is known as the hip depth and, as already stated, is usually 8"-9" (20.3cm-22.9cm). Still holding the hip m/ment tape in position, use the other end of the tape to measure from the waist to the tape measure at hip level.

6 Upper hip
If the figure is large or if the proportions of hips and waist differ considerably from normal, take the upper hip m/ment approx. 4" (10.2cm) below the waist. This is also helpful when drawing the curve of the side seam of a skirt between hips and waist. The upper hip line should then be drawn on the skirt block and the m/ment checked.

7 Back waist length
Measured from the small prominent bone at the back of the neck to the tape at the waist. When measuring for a one-piece dress, jacket or coat (i.e. one without a seam at the waist) also take the total length m/ment at this stage.

8 Front waist length
Measured from the base of the neck at the centre front to the tape at the waist. The back waist length should be approximately 1½" (3.8cm) longer than the front waist length.

9 Bust point length
This measurement is essential as it determines the angle and position of the bust dart. Figures may vary considerably in this m/ment, which is taken from the tape at the waist up to the bust point.

10 Back width
Measured across the back from armhole to armhole, approximately 4" (10.2cm) below the back of the neck. (If the person being measured is not wearing a garment with an armhole seam, the correct position of the seam must be estimated.)

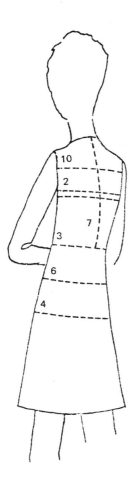

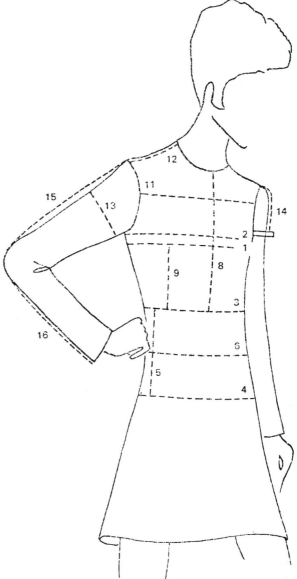

11 Front width
Measured at the same level as the back width: approximately 1½" (3.8cm) below the base of the neck at the centre front.
(Various other terms are used to describe these two m/ments.)

12 Shoulders
Measured from the side of the neck to the end of the shoulder bone.

The shape and position of the armhole seam, which contributes a great deal to the finished appearance of the garment, is dependent on the accuracy of the last three m/ments, although some practice is needed to take them accurately.

13 Top arm girth
This m/ment is taken around the widest part of the arm, approx. 6" (15.2cm) below the shoulder point.

When taking the following 3 m/ments, the end of the tape should be held so that it rests on the top of the shoulder bone. Continue to hold the tape in the same position while taking all three.

14 Depth of sleevehead
To take this m/ment, place a ruler as high as possible under the arm of the person being measured and measure from the shoulder bone to the upper edge of the ruler.

15 Elbow point length
Measured from the shoulder bone to the point of the elbow *with the arm bent.*

16 Sleeve length
Continue holding the tape measure in the same position as for the above m/ment and measure to just below the small bone on the outside of the wrist, *with the arm straight.*

Skirt
Waist, hip and hip depth m/ments are taken as for a dress.

17 Front length
Measured from the tape at the c/f waist to the ground, noting the length of skirt required. Allow the tape to hang naturally—do not stretch it. Deduct the length of skirt required from the ground length, and that amount is then deducted from the back and side ground lengths to find the skirt lengths at those points.

18 Back length
Measured from the tape at the c/b waist to the ground.

19 Side length
Measured from the tape at the side of the waist, over the prominence of the hip, to the ground. (Should be used as a check m/ment if the figure has prominent hips.)

Trousers

Waist, hip and hip depth m/ments are taken as for a dress and skirt.

All the following m/ments are taken standing at the side of the figure:

20 Crotch depth

This m/ment is taken with the person sitting on a firm chair or the edge of a table, from the tape at the side of the waist over the hip prominence to the surface of the chair.

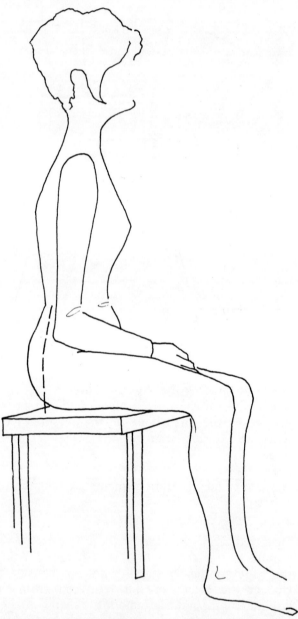

21 Outside leg length

Measured from the tape at the side of the waist to the length required, which is usually just below the ankle bone. Remember to allow for the heel height which will be worn.

22 Knee level

Measured from the tape at the side of the waist to the side of the knee. The widths of trousers at knee and ankle bear so little relation to body m/ments that there is no need to measure them.

Ease

The amounts of ease shown on the m/ment chart are the average amounts used at the moment for a dress in a material of average thickness. A coat or jacket would need approximately twice these amounts (see page 49 for coat blocks). All circumference m/ments must have ease added as a garment made exactly to the m/ments of the figure would be very uncomfortable to wear. The only length m/ments which have ease added are: depth of sleeve head, to allow room for the arm to move, sleeve length, to allow for the elbow to bend, and crotch depth, to allow ease of movement in trousers.

½" (13mm) is added to the back width line, although not to the front width line. This is because arm movements are usually forward and upwards, but rarely back. The 1" (2.5cm) ease allowed at the waist is the usual amount allowed on a skirt or trousers, or for a close-fitting dress with a waist seam. Most dresses without waist seams have considerably more ease than this: 6"-8" (15.2cm-20.3cm) is the usual amount for a loose fitting blouse or dress.

Measurement Chart

Dress Measurements	Body Measure	Ease	Total	Half Total
1. Bust		2″/5.0cm		
2. High bust		2″/5.0cm		
3. Waist		1″/2.5cm (skirt)		
4. Hip		2″/5.0cm		
5. Hip depth				
6. Upper Hip		2″/5.0cm		
7. Back waist length				
8. Front waist length				
9. Bust point				
10. Back width		½″/13mm		
11. Front width				
12. Shoulder				
Sleeve Measurements				
13. Top arm		2″/5.0cm		
14. Depth of sleevehead		½″/13mm		
15. Sleeve length		½″/13mm		
16. Elbow point length				
Skirt Measurements				
17. Front length				
18. Back length				
19. Side length				
Trouser Measurements				
20. Crotch depth				
21. Outside length				

Bodice Blocks

Construction lines
(These are shown throughout as broken lines on the diagrams.)

Draw a rectangle measuring half of bust m/ment plus 1" (2.5cm), by back waist m/ment.

The left hand edge will be the centre back line and the right hand edge the centre front line. The lower line will be referred to as the waist line for the moment, although the true waist line will be curved. Letter the rectangle A-B-C-D as shown.

From A measure down half of back waist length plus 1" (2.5cm) and mark point E. Square across and mark point F on the centre front line. (In sizes 16 and 18 add 1¼" (3.1cm) instead of 1" (2.5cm), and in size 20 and larger add 1½" (3.8cm).) Calculate one-quarter of the back waist length and draw a line this distance below the top line (G-H). This is the back width and front width line.

Draw a vertical line mid-way between the c/b and the c/f, then draw a line parallel to this and ½" (13mm) towards the c/b (J-K). The first line represents the true side of the figure; the second is the side seam line.

Block lines
Back
Neckline
Measure one-sixth of back width m/ment along the top line from A. Square up ½" (13mm) and mark the neck point (L).
(In sizes 16 and 18, square up ⅝" (16mm) and in size 20 and larger square up ¾" (19mm).)
Curve the neckline from L to A as shown.

Shoulder
Measure half of the back width m/ment plus ¼" (6mm) along the back width line from G and mark point M. Square up half of A-G plus ¼" (6mm) from M and mark point N. Extend the line N-M approx. 2" (5.0cm) below M as a guide for drawing the a/h curve.

Join L-N for the shoulder line, extending it 1" (2.5cm) beyond N. Add 1" (2.5cm) to the shoulder m/ment of the figure and measure this amount from L to mark the shoulder point (P). (The 1" (2.5cm) is made up by ¼" (6mm) ease and ¾" (19mm) allowance for the shoulder dart.)

The shoulder point (P) must always be at least ¼" (6mm) beyond N to give a slight curve to the top of the a/h, but figures vary so much in their proportion of shoulder width to back width that this may not always occur; if necessary make the dart wider, although not wider than 1" (2.5cm).

If this is still insufficient, make two darts and transfer one to the neckline (see page 24), although if the m/ments vary a great deal from average it would be advisable to remeasure the figure.

Shoulder dart
Mark point Q mid-way between L and P and join it to the centre point of the back width line (G-M). Make the dart 3" (7.6cm) long and ¾" (19mm) wide by measuring from Q towards the cb. Raise point Q ½" (13mm) and join to P. Make the other side of the dart the same length and join to L. (Raising point Q ½" (13mm) ensures that the shoulder seam will be a straight line after the dart has been sewn.)

Armhole
Draw the a/h curve P-M-J, although the curve may only be provisional until the front block has been drafted. Then the entire curve may be drawn, thus ensuring that the back and front a/h curves will join smoothly.

Side seam
Measure ¾" (19mm) from K towards the cb line and mark point R. Join R-J with a slightly curved line (to avoid reducing the width of the block at bust level.) Extend the line slightly below the waist line.

Waist line
Measure ½" (13mm) down from R and curve to B for the true waist line.

Waist dart
From B, measure half of G-M along the waist line and square up to the u/arm line. Measure ½" (13mm) each side of this line to form the dart, as shown.

(The m/ment of the waist line of the block, less the dart, should equal one-quarter of the waist m/ment of the figure. If necessary, adjust the width of the dart.)

Front
Neckline
The width of the front neckline is the same as that of the back neckline — one-sixth of the back width m/ment measured along the top line from D (point S). Measure the same amount plus ½" (13mm) down from D and mark point T.* Square up ½" (13mm) from S (point U) and curve the neckline provisionally from U to T as shown.*

Shoulder
Draw a short construction line 1½" (3.8cm) below the top line as shown. Measure the shoulder m/ment of the figure from U onto this line and mark the shoulder point (V). Join U-V for the shoulder line. Also draw the centralised shoulder line as a guide: measure ½" (13mm) below U and ¾" (19mm) below V and join with a broken line as shown.

Armhole
Measure half of the front width m/ment of the figure along the front width line from H and mark

point W. Curve the a/h V-W-J ensuring that it joins smoothly to the back a/h curve. (Note that the lowest point of the a/h curve is on the broken line, not the side seam, since that is the true side of the figure.)

Side seam
Extend the line J-K ½" (13mm) below K and mark point X.

Waist line
Measure the front waist length of the figure down from T along the cf and mark point Y. Curve from X to Y for the waist line.

Bust point and bust line
Draw the dart line parallel to the cf and approx. 4" (10.2cm) from it (half the distance between the bust points of the figure). Extend the line from point Z on the waist line up to the u/arm line. From Z, measure the bust point length of the figure along the dart line and mark the bust point (B.P.). Draw the

bust line on front and back blocks, passing through the bust point and parallel to the u/arm line.

Waist dart
The waist line of the front block, less the dart, should equal one-quarter of the waist m/ment of the figure, plus ½" (13mm). Calculate this amount and subtract it from the m/ment of the line X-Y. The remainder forms the dart. Measure half of the dart width each side of Z and join to the bust point. As with the shoulder dart, one side of the waist dart will be shorter than the other. Extend the shorter side to match the longer and re-draw the waist line curve.

Cutting out the blocks
Cut all straight lines first — shoulder, side seams, c/b and c/f. Place shoulder seams together to check that the neck and a/h curves are continuous and place side seams together to check that a/h and waist curves are continuous. Correct if necessary before cutting along the curves. Make balance marks on the shoulder seam by matching first the neckline curves, then the a/h curves to make a balance mark each side of the dart.

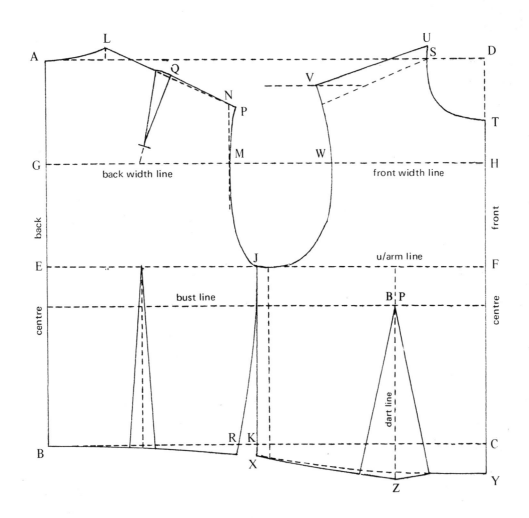

Sleeve Block

Construction lines

Draw a rectangle measuring top arm girth plus 2" (5.0cm) by sleeve length.

Divide the rectangle vertically into 4 equal sections (folding the paper to make crease lines is the simplest method).

Name and letter the lines as follows: line AB is the centre line, line CD is the back arm line and line EF is the front arm line. The lower line will be referred to as the wrist line, although the true wrist line will be curved.

Measure the depth of sleeve head plus ½" (13mm) down from A and square across for the underarm line (GH). Measure the elbow point length from A on to the back arm line and mark the elbow point (J). Square across for the elbow line (KL).

Block lines
Sleevehead

From E, measure down half the distance between top line and underarm line (M).

From C, measure down the same amount less ½" (13mm) (N).

The s/h is curved between the five points G-N-A-M-H but guide lines are necessary to draw a good curve. Join G-N, N-A, A-M, and M-H. Mark the centre of each line and square out the following amounts: between G and N – ½" (13mm), between N and A – ½" (13mm), between A and M – 1" (2.5cm) and between M and H – ¾" (19mm). There are now nine points to guide the curve of the s/h. Note that the curves of the front s/h are more pronounced than those of the back: the upper curve to allow ease over the shoulder bone and the lower to allow the arm to be moved forward easily.

Wrist line

Measure down ½" (13mm) from D and up ½" (13mm) up from F. Curve the true wrist line as shown.

Cutting out

Cut out the block along the side seams, then fold the paper along the lines C-D and E-F so that the side seams are together. Check that the curves of s/h and wrist are continuous across the seam and correct them if necessary.

Balance points

The balance points, which show how the s/h joins to the a/h, are the points M and N on the s/h.

After cutting out the bodice and sleeve blocks, place the back s/h face downwards against the back a/h with curves together and the sleeve seam ½" (13mm) beyond the bodice side seam (i.e. level with the *true* side of the bodice). Move the s/h around the a/h, keeping the curves together, until the balance point (N) is reached. Mark the corresponding point on the a/h.

Repeat the procedure with the front block, placing the sleeve to the *broken* line at the side of the bodice block (i.e. to the *true* side of the bodice) and mark the front balance point. Each balance point should be approx. 1" (2.5cm) below the back width or front width line.

It is very important that balance points are marked on the blocks and transferred to all patterns made from the blocks. They must then be transferred to the fabric after cutting.

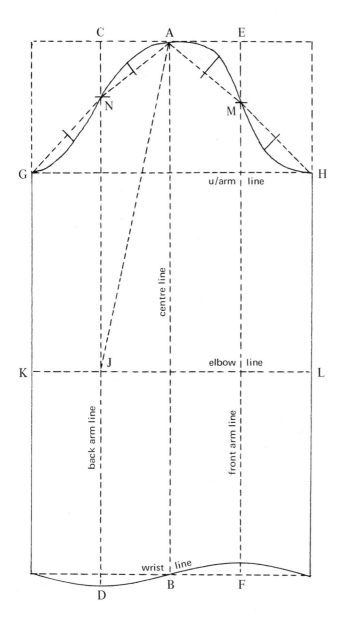

Skirt Blocks

Construction lines

Draw a rectangle measuring half of hip m/ment plus 2" (5.0cm), by front skirt length.

(As on the bodice blocks, the left hand edge of the rectangle will be the c/b and the right hand edge will be the c/f.)

Draw the hip line by measuring the hip depth less ½" (13mm) down from the top line and squaring across. Name the hip line.

Back

Block lines
Waist line

Measure one-quarter of waist m/ment plus 1" (2.5cm) from A along the top line (B). Square up ½" (13mm) from B (C). Curve from A to C for the waist line.

Waist dart

The best position for the waist dart in the back of a skirt is approx. 3" (7.6cm) from the c/b, although it may be slightly further in larger sizes. Darts which are further apart than this will not be pointing towards the fullest part of the seat. Measure 3" (7.6cm) from the c/b along the waistline (D) and square down 5" (12.7cm) from the curve (E). Measure ½" (13mm) each side of D and join to E.

Side seam

Measure one-quarter of hip m/ment from the c/b along the hip line (F). Square down from F to the hem line (G).

Measure out ½" (13mm) from G (H) and join H-F. Continue the line above F for approx 4" (10.2cm) to serve as a guide for drawing the upper part of the side seam, between F and C. The curve should follow the straight line for 2"-3" (5.0cm-7.6cm) and then curve to C, thus allowing sufficient room for the curve of the hip bones.

Hemline

Measure up $\frac{1}{8}$" (3mm) from H and measure down ½" (13mm) from the c/b, or as required, according to back skirt length. Curve the hemline as shown.

Front

Waistline

Measure one-quarter of waist m/ment plus 1¼" (3.1cm) from J along the top line from the c/f line (K). Square up ½" (13mm) (L) and measure down ½" (13mm) from J (M). Curve from L to M for the waistline.

Waist dart

The front waist dart should be approx. 5" (12.7cm) from the c/f (not less as its purpose is to provide shaping for the hip bones and many blocks place this dart too close to the c/f). Like the back dart, it should be at right angles to the waist curve but considerably shorter, approx. 3" (7.6cm).

Measure 5" (12.7cm) along the waistline from the c/f (N). Square down 3" (7.6cm) from the curve and mark the base of the dart (P). Measure $\frac{3}{8}$" (9mm) each side of N and join to P.

Side seam

Measure one-quarter of hip m/ment plus 1" (2.55cm) along the hip line from the c/f (Q). Square down from Q to the hemline (R). Measure out ½" (13mm) from R (point H, as on the back block), and join Q-H for the side seam. Continue the line above the hip line, as on the back, and curve from Q to L.

Hemline

Measure up $\frac{1}{8}$" (3mm) at H and curve to the c/f.

This block has ½" (13mm) added to the side seam on back and front (i.e. the total hem width is 2" (5.0cm) greater than the hip m/ment). This is the minimum hem width for any skirt, even if it is intended to appear completely straight, as otherwise it will appear to taper inwards.

If a slightly flared skirt is required, some fullness may be added at the side seams (and the line joined to just above the hip line to ensure a good line) but no more than 1½" (3.8cm) should be added at each seam as a larger amount would cause the fullness to hang in folds at the sides instead of being evenly distributed around the skirt. This is a very serious fault in skirt cutting. If greater fullness is required, the block must be cut and spread apart as shown on pages 155 & 156.

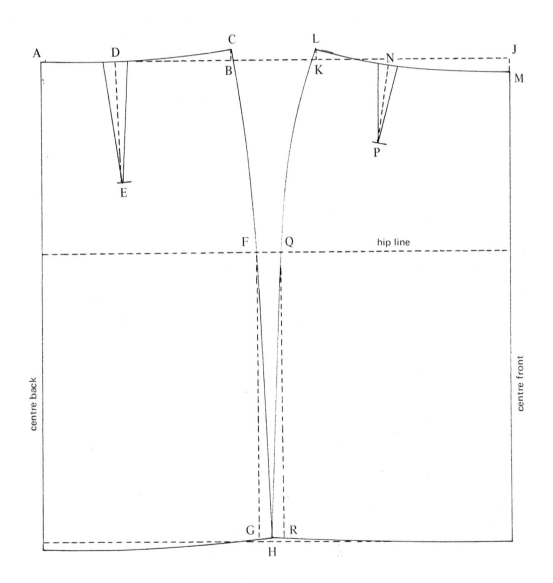

Trouser Blocks

The trousers produced by these instructions are close fitting over the hips and thighs and fall straight from thigh to ankle with a hem width of half hip m/ment plus 1" (2.5cm). This shape has been chosen as being the easiest to adapt to the shape required by adding or subtracting width at the knee and ankle (see page 169-171).

The blocks are constructed by drafting the front block, tracing it on to a new sheet of paper and using it as a basis for drafting the back block. It is very important that the crease lines are marked clearly as they control the balance of the trousers.

Construction lines

Draw a rectangle measuring one-quarter of hip m/ment, plus ½" (13mm), by trouser length required (the right hand edge is the c/f line and should be at least 3" (7.6cm) from the edge of the paper).

Draw the hip line by measuring the hip depth down from the top line and squaring across. Draw the crotch line by measuring the crotch depth plus ½" (13mm) down from the top line and squaring across.

Draw the thigh line 3" (7.6cm) below the crotch line.

Draw the knee line according to the knee length m/ment.

Name all the lines.

Front

Waistline

Measure down ½" (13mm) from the top line and mark point A. Measure one-quarter of waist m/ment plus 1" (2.5cm) along the top line (B) and curve from B to A. Draw the waist dart — 5" (12.7cm) from the c/f, 3" (7.6cm) long, ¾" (19mm) wide and at right angles to the waistline.

Centre front seam

Mark point C at the junction of the c/f line and the crotch line and extend the crotch line beyond the c/f line. Extend the hip, thigh and knee lines. Measure one-twelfth of hip m/ment less ¾" (19mm) from C and mark point D. Draw a short construction line from C at 45° to C-D as shown and measure half of C-D plus ½" (13mm) (point E). Curve the c/f seam A-E-D keeping it on the line A-C for 3"-4" (7.6cm-10.2cm).

Inside leg seam

Mark point F where the c/f line crosses the knee line and measure out half of C-D (point G).

Mark point H where the c/f line crosses the

ankle line and measure out half of C-D (point J).

Join J-G and continue the line above G for 4"-5" (10.2cm-12.7cm) as a guide, then curve to D.

Outside leg seam

Mark point K where the hip line meets the side line.

Calculate half of hip m/ment plus 1" (2.5cm). Measure half of that amount along the knee line from G (point L). Measure the same amount along the ankle line from J (point M). Join M-L and continue the line above L for approx. 3"-4" (7.6cm-10.2cm) as a guide. Curve to K and B.

(This curve, and that of the inside leg seam between G and D, may be adjusted slightly according to the width desired on thigh and crotch lines but it must always curve smoothly.)

Crease line

Mark the centre point of the ankle and knee lines, join and continue to the waist.

Hem line

Measure ¼" (6mm) above the ankle line on the crease line and curve to M and J.

Cut out the front trouser block, place it face downwards on a new sheet of paper and trace, allowing a margin of 3" (7.6cm) all round. Re-draw all the construction lines and name them and letter all points as on the front block. The lower part of the back pattern, below the knee line, is the same as the front, except for the curve of the hemline.

Back

C/b seam

Measure out ¼" (6mm) from D along the crotch line and mark point N.

Mark point P where the crease line meets the front waist line. Measure 1" (2.5cm) from P towards A and mark point Q. Square up 1½" (3.8cm) from Q (point R). Join R-C as a guide line. Measure half of crotch depth from R and mark point S. The c/b seam is curved R-S-E-N. It should be hollowed slightly between R and S and should pass through or just below point E.

Waistline

Measure one-quarter waist plus 1" (2.5cm) from R on to the top line (T) and curve as shown.

Waist dart

Draw the waist dart — 3" (7.6cm) from the c/b, 5" (12.7cm) long, at right angles to the waist line and ¾" (19mm) wide.

Outside leg seam

Measure out ¾" (19mm) from K (point U). Curve from L to U and join to T. (T-U will be almost a straight line.)

Inside leg seam

Curve from G to N as shown.

Hemline

Measure down ½" (13mm) from the ankle line along the crease line and curve to M and J.

Place the blocks together at the top of the inside leg seam to check that the centre seam is a continuous curve and place them together at the top of the outside leg seam to check the waistline curve. Place each of the seams together at the hem to check the hem curve.

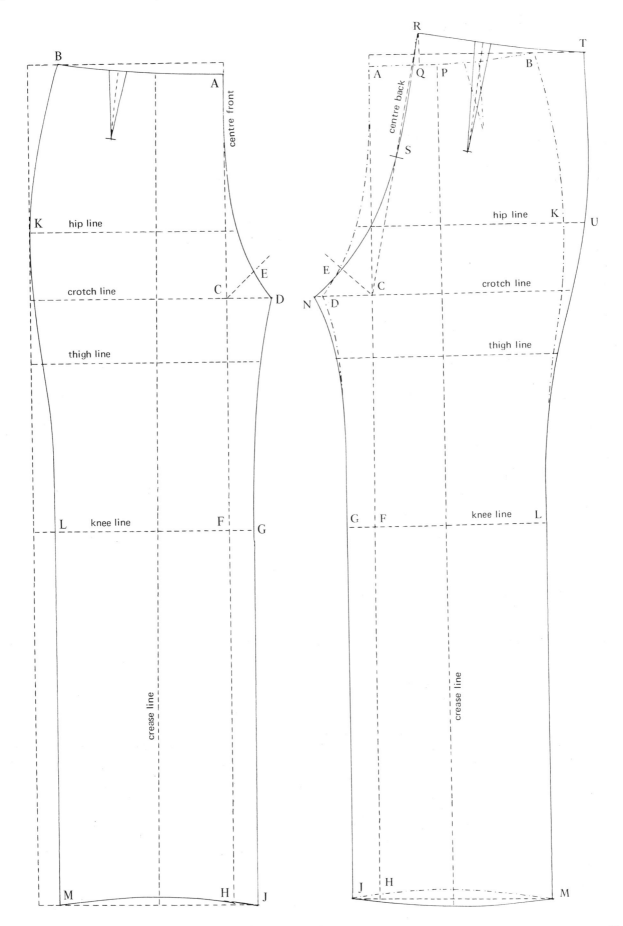

Children's Blocks

The children's blocks are constructed in a very similar way to the adults' blocks. There are no skirt blocks as children seldom wear close fitting skirts but if a skirt block is required the adult's block may be used. The children's sleeve block, like the adult's, is long and loose fitting for ease of adaptation.

Bodice blocks
Construction lines
Draw a rectangle measuring half of chest m/ment plus 1" (2.5cm), by back waist length. (This allows 2" (5.0cm) ease on the complete block but more may be added if required.)

Letter the rectangle A-B-C-D as shown. The left hand edge will be the c/b line and the right hand edge the c/f line. The lower line will be referred to as the waist line for the moment, although the true waist line will be curved.

From A, measure down half of back waist length plus ¼" (6mm) (E) and square across (F) for the u/arm line. (For size 10 and above add $\frac{3}{8}$" (9mm) instead of ¼" (6mm).)

Draw another line mid-way between the top line and the u/arm line (G-H). This is the back width and front width line.

Draw a vertical line from the u/arm line down to the waist midway between the c/b and c/f lines (J-K).

Pattern lines
Neckline
Measure one-sixth of the back width m/ment of the figure along the top line from A. Square up ¼" (6mm) for the neck point (L). (For size 10 and above, square up $\frac{3}{8}$" (9mm).)

Curve the neckline from L to A as shown.

Shoulder
Measure half of the back width m/ment of the figure plus ¼" (6mm) along the back width line from G (M). Calculate half of A-G and square up this distance plus ¼" (6mm) from M(N). Join L-N and extend the line slightly beyond N. From L, measure the shoulder m/ment of the figure, plus ¼" (6mm) for ease, along the shoulder line and mark the shoulder point (P). P must be slightly beyond N to give a good curve to the a/h and if this does not occur a shoulder dart should be made as for the adult block (page 10). Curve the a/h P-M-J.

Side seam
Measure ½" (13mm) from K towards the c/b (Q) and curve from Q to J. Extend the line slightly below the waistline.

Waistline
Measure ¼" (6mm) down from Q and curve to B.

Waist dart
From B, measure half of G-M along the waist line (R) and square up to the u/arm line. Make a dart ¾" (19mm) wide at R.

Front bodice block

Neckline
Make the front neckline $\frac{1}{8}$" (3mm) wider than the back neckline to allow a small amount of extra ease at the front of the bodice. Square up as for the back neckline (point S). The depth of the neckline, which is measured along the c/f line from D, is the same as the width of the back neckline. Curve the neckline as shown.

Shoulder
Draw a construction line 1" (2.5cm) below the top line.

Measure the shoulder m/ment of the figure from S on to the construction line and mark point T.

Armhole
Measure half of the front width m/ment of the figure along the front width line and mark point U. Curve the a/h T-U-J, hollowing the curve at the base of the a/h more than for the back a/h.

Side seam
Measure ½" (13mm) from K towards the c/f (V) and curve from J to V, extending the line slightly below the waistline.

Waist line
Measure ¼" (6mm) down from V and mark point W. Measure the front waist length of the figure along the c/f from the base of the neckline and mark the c/f waist point (X). Curve from W to X for the true waist line.

Chest line
Calculate half of G-E and measure that amount down from E on the c/b. Square across from the c/b for the chest line.

Waist dart
Mark a point midway between J and F and measure 1" (2.5cm) towards the c/f (Y). Square down from Y to the waist line (Z) and make a dart at Z, extending to the chest line. The dart should be ¾" (19mm) wide, or as required, in order that the waist line of the block measures half of the waist m/ment of the figure, plus ½" (13mm).

In sizes 1-10, the *back* dart should be made wider if any adjustment is needed; in sizes 12 and 14, the *front* dart should be the wider.

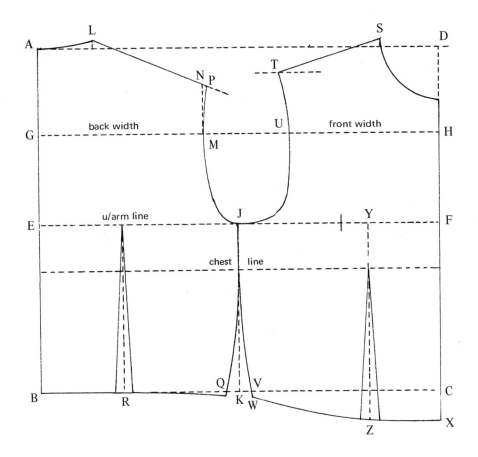

Children's sleeve block

Construction lines

Draw a rectangle A-B-C-D measuring top arm m/ment plus 2" (5.0cm), by sleeve length. Divide the rectangle vertically into four equal sections and name the back arm line (E-F), the centre line (G-H), and the front arm line (J-K).

Measure the depth of s/h down from the top line and square across for the u/arm line (L-M).

Measure the elbow point length from G on to the back arm line (N) and square across for the elbow line. (This line is only needed when a long, close-fitting sleeve is to be made.)

Pattern lines
Sleevehead

Measure down half of the depth of s/h from J (point P) and measure the same amount plus ¼" (6mm) from E (point Q) (⅜" (9mm) in size 8 and above). The s/h is curved through the five points L-Q-G-P-M.

Wrist

Measure down ⅜" (9mm) on the back arm line and measure up ¼" (6mm) on the front arm line. Curve the wrist line as shown.

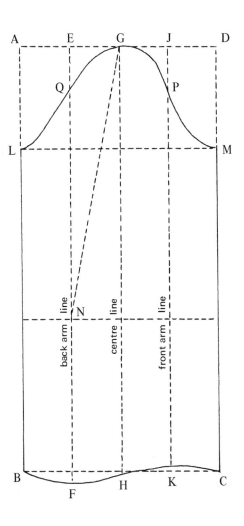

Making a Pattern

The sketch or photograph on which the pattern is going to be based must always be kept within sight while the pattern is being cut. The first step is to analyse the design with regard to the method of dart shaping (see pages 25-39). If there are seams passing over the bust point, the shaping may be incorporated in them; if not, decide on the position for the dart.

The procedure for making a pattern can most easily be described by listing the order of work with reference to the appropriate section. Omit those parts of the order of work which do not apply to the design being cut.

1 Outline the front and back bodice blocks.
2 Adapt the blocks to coat blocks if making a coat or jacket (page 49).
3 Add an allowance for overlap and facing at c/f or c/b if the bodice is to have an opening with buttons and buttonholes (pages 51–56).
4 Adapt to kimono or raglan styles if required.
5 Draw decorative seams, i.e. seams which do not contain any of the dart shaping, such as a yoke seam or waistband.
6 Decide on the position for the dart shaping and the method of using it (pages 25-39), i.e. as a dart or concealed in a seam or gathers, etc. If the design has fullness, any flat sections, such as a yoke, should be cut away before the dart is transferred (page 28). Transfer all or part of the waist dart to the new position, as required.
7 Draw the new neckline and tighten it if necessary (see page 45).
8 If the garment is sleeveless, tighten the a/h as shown on page 47.
9 Adapt the front and back bodice to a one-piece dress (page 41) or Princess dress (page 43) if required.
10 Make the collar pattern (page 73).
11 Outline the sleeve block.
12 Adapt the shape of the s/h area if required—drop-shoulder (page 128) extra fullness (pages 100-114) etc.
13 Adapt to deep a/h, shallow s/h, etc. if required.
14 Adapt to the required width at the wrist—tight fitting, bishop, etc (pages 96-100).
15 Outline the skirt blocks.
16 Draw the yoke seam, if any, and cut the yoke away before adapting the remainder of the block (page 163).
17 Adapt the block according to the hem width, shape and seaming required (pages 148-168).

Bodices

Shoulder and side seams centralized
Dart positions
Yoked styles
Inset waistband
Panel seams
One-piece dress
Princess line dress
Low necklines
Sleeveless styles
Coat blocks

Shoulder and Side Seam

As already explained in the section on drafting the blocks, the shoulder and side seams of the blocks used here are set back: the side seam by ½" (13mm) and the shoulder seam by ½" (13mm) at the neck point and ¾" (19mm) at the shoulder point. For some adaptations it is necessary to centralise the seams, e.g. raglan sleeves, capes.

Outline the bodice blocks.

Back
Add ½" (13mm) at the neck point and ¾" (19mm) at the shoulder point and join to form the new shoulder seam. Extend the dart line A-B to join the new shoulder seam (C). From C measure the width of the original dart towards the shoulder point (D) and join A-D. Thus the dart is the same width as in the original seam. *(Diag 1)*
 Add ½" (13mm) to the side seam, curving the line to match the original.

Front
Cut away the same amounts from shoulder and side seams as were added to the back block. *(Diag 2)*
Place the blocks with shoulder points and shoulder seams together to check the curve of the a/h.

The side seams of the skirt block may occasionally need to be centralised, e.g. when making a four-panelled skirt pattern or a one piece dress with kimono sleeves. Add ½" (13mm) to the side seam of the back block and cut away ½" (13mm) from the front side seam.

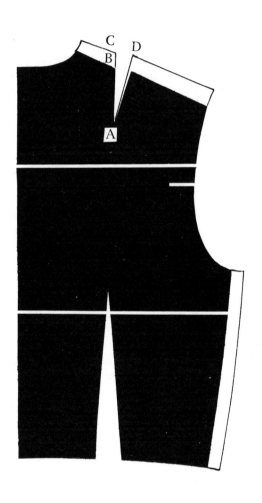

diag 1

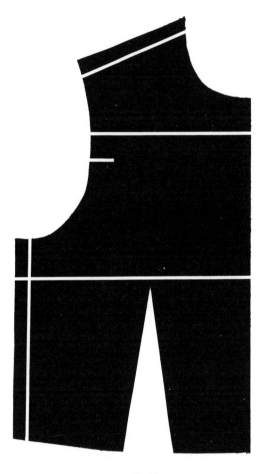

diag 2

Dart Positions

It is convenient for the dart shaping to be shown on the block as one large dart at the waist, but it would not be advisable for the dart to be sewn in that position as such a large dart would distort the grain of the bodice and 'poke' at the bust point, due to the wide angle between fold and stitching line. In some dress styles it is not possible for the entire dart to be sewn at the waist, e.g. in a one-piece dress (page 41). It is therefore advisable to make two smaller darts by moving part of the waist dart to another position.

Diag 1 shows the possible positions for the dart: shoulder, neckline, armhole, any position on the c/f seam, any position on the side seam. In fact, theoretically, the dart may point from any position on each of the edges of the block, although some positions give a more attractive shape than others. For instance, a dart from the side seam should slant upwards, even if only very slightly, as this is more flattering than a straight or downwards slanting dart. A shoulder dart usually begins from the centre of the shoulder, or closer to the neck, as a dart from too near the a/h would make the garment appear to be slipping off the shoulders. A dart from the a/h is not usually attractive as it often indicates that the pattern was badly cut, resulting in a loose a/h which had to be darted to fit. A neckline dart or a dart from the c/f seam, however, may be made decorative by tucking or stitching to give a sun-ray effect.

In theory, a dart from any position will ensure the same fit but in practice certain positions are more suitable for certain figure types. For example, a shoulder dart, and to a lesser extent a neckline dart, give more scope for fitting a figure with a large bust and narrow shoulders or a figure which is hollow above the bust. Dart shaping can also be concealed in seams which form part of the design of the garment, the only condition being that the seam must pass over, or very close to, the bust point in order that the fullness provided for the bust by the dart is correctly positioned. Examples of this are the standard panel seam and shoulder panel seam shown on pages 36-39. A panel seam may also be drawn from the neckline. A dress or coat without a seam at the waist and with panel seams from the a/h at back and front is called a Princess line. This gives a smooth, neatly fitting line and can be fitted very closely to the waist if desired, due to the number of seams.

The dart shaping may also be partly concealed in a seam and partly visible, such as the panel seam with dart on page 39 or the yoke on page 30 in which the dart shaping is used as gathers. These are seams which pass close to the bust point but not sufficiently close for the shaping to be entirely incorporated in them. When cutting the pattern for such a style, the 'flat' part, i.e. the yoke or side panel, must be cut away before the dart is transferred. If this principle is followed, even the most complicated styles can be easily cut.

When the waist dart is closed and a new dart opened in another position, the new dart may not be the same width as the original although it will contain exactly the same amount of shaping. This

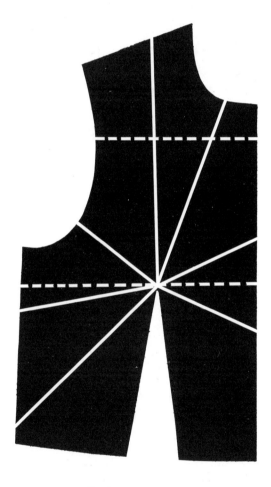

diag 1

loose styles, but the latter can rarely dispense with darts altogether. The exception is a style with a bias-cut bodice in which the fabric may be eased and shrunk to provide the necessary shaping, but this is only possible in a small size and at couture standards of workmanship. Darts are seldom decorative but are essential to make the garment fit and a skilful pattern cutter will attempt to distribute the dart shaping so that the darts appear smaller and less conspicuous. The least conspicuous position for a dart is from the side seam (known as an u/arm dart) and for this reason it is the position most frequently used. Very long darts drawn from the waist or below are known as French darts (page 27). A French dart is very flattering and enables the bodice to be fitted more closely under the bust by curving the sides of the dart. The least conspicuous dart of all is an u/arm dart drawn to slant very slightly upwards so that it is concealed by the arm most of the time. The most conspicuous is the shoulder dart, unless it can be concealed by a large collar. The waist dart is also conspicuous as it is close to the c/f, but it is less so as it is under, rather than over, the prominence of the bust. Most panel seams are conspicuous because by definition they must pass over the bust point, but those which are combined with a dart, such as the example on page 39, are far less conspicuous.

Usually approximately half of the waist dart is transferred so that the bust shaping is evenly divided between the two darts, but the amount may be varied according to the design of the garment and the total amount of shaping required: from one-quarter of the dart, or less, to three-quarters of it. The dart remaining at the waist will be used if the bodice is to be close-fitting at the waist, but it may be made narrower or omitted altogether if a loose-fitting dress is required (see one-piece dress on page 41). It should be straightened before it is used, as shown on the following page, diag 3.

It is a very simple process to change the position of a dart and involves drawing a line in the position that the new dart is required, cutting along the line and folding out part of the waist dart so that a dart opens along the new line (see following page).

Although the dart on the block extends to the bust point, the darts on a pattern must be shortened 1"-2" (2.5cm-5.0cm) to allow a little more ease over the bust point, to prevent the dart 'poking' and to make it less conspicuous. The exact amount by which a dart is shortened depends on personal preference and the size of the dart; a narrow dart can be shortened more than a wide dart.

(For the sake of clarity, all darts are shown as cut away in the diagrams. It is usual for darts to be cut away on *blocks* to enable them to be outlined but not on patterns as it is then easier for them to be folded out.)

is because darts opening from the different points vary in length when measured from the bust point. The longer the dart, the wider it will be. Think of it as a triangle which is being extended at its base—the base must become wider.

Close fitting styles need more dart shaping than

Underarm dart (diags 1, 2 and 3)

An u/arm dart may be drawn from any point on the side seam but is more flattering if it slants upwards slightly.

Diag 1—Outline the front bodice block. Measure down 1" (2.5cm) (or as required) from the bust line along the side seam and mark point A. Join A to the bust point (B) to form the dart line. Draw the centre line of the waist dart, B-C. Mark point D as shown.

Diag 2—Cut along the dart line. Fold the pattern along the left hand edge of the waist dart (the line B-D) and place point D to point C. Half of the dart shaping has now been transferred into the u/arm dart which has opened at A, and this process is known as 'folding out' the dart. A larger or smaller amount of shaping may be transferred by folding out more or less than half of the waist dart.

Diag 3—The centre line of the new waist dart is now at an angle to the c/f and the dart may be straightened if required by drawing a new centre line, B—E parallel to the c/f, and measuring half of the new width of the dart each side of E. Shorten the dart at the same time by measuring 1½" (3.8cm) down from B (point F) and joining the sides of the new dart to F. (The solid lines in diag 3 show the straightened dart.) Alternatively, the dart may be drawn with the right hand edge parallel to the c/f, depending on the effect required.

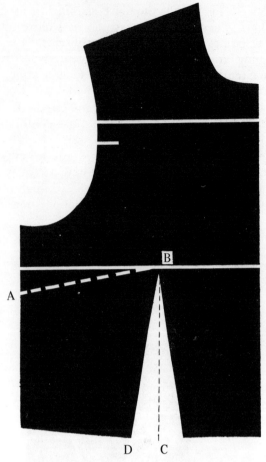

diag 1

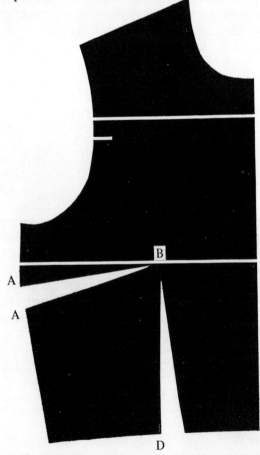

diag 2

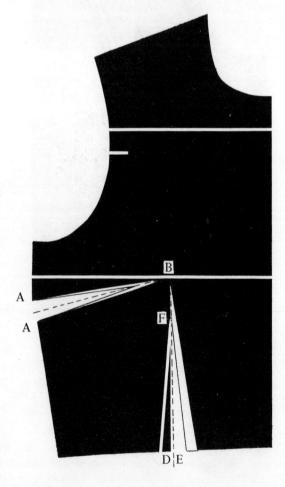

diag 3

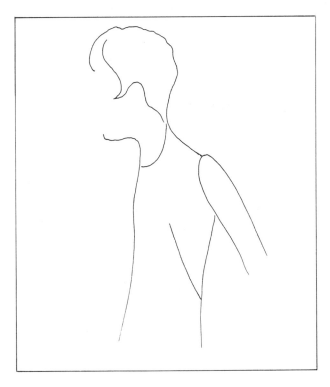

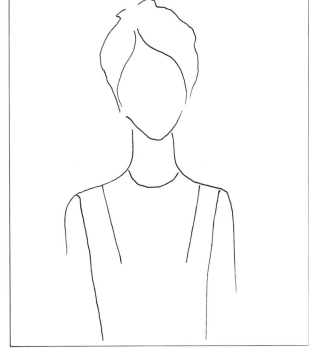

French dart (diag 4)

The French dart is a variation on the u/arm dart but is drawn from a lower point on the side seam and is often curved. Curve from the required position on the side seam to the bust point and cut along the curve. Fold out part of the waist dart as required, straighten and shorten the waist dart and shorten the French dart carefully, retaining the smooth curve. The edges of the dart may be curved outwards slightly to make the bodice closer fitting between bust and waist.

Shoulder dart (diag 5)

Mark the centre point of the shoulder and measure ½" (13mm) towards the neck point. This is the usual line but may be varied according to preference. The line may also be curved. Cut along the dart line and transfer part of the waist dart. Straighten the waist dart and shorten both darts.

This same method is used to transfer the waist dart to any other position.

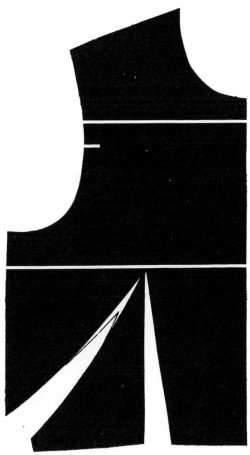

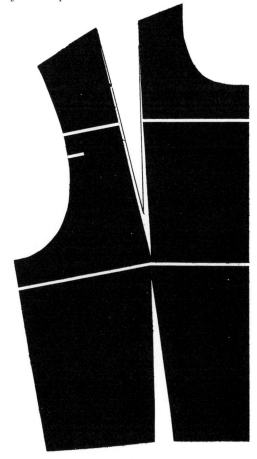

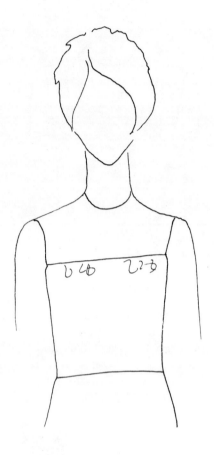

Diags 1-5 show three methods of adapting the block to simple yoked styles by transferring the waist dart into the yoke seam. The yoke line may be straight, curved or pointed, and the fullness may be gathered, pleated, tucked or darted into the yoke.

Diag 1
Outline the front bodice block and draw the yoke line in the required position. Mark balance points. Continue the centre line of the dart upwards to the yoke line (A). Measure 1'' (2.5cm) each side of A (B and C) and join B and C to the bust point.

Diag 2
Cut the yoke away and cut from A, B and C to within $\frac{1}{8}$'' (3mm) of the bust point. Fold out all or part of the waist dart and divide the fullness equally between the three positions. Correct the yoke line, which will now be curved. The fullness should not extend nearer to the a/h than the balance point.

The back pattern may be made in the same way.

Diags 3 and 4: Yoked style with added fullness
Outline the front bodice block. Draw the yoke line in the required position and mark balance points. Divide the yoke line into four (A,B,C) and the waist into three, disregarding the dart, (D,E). Join A-D and C-E and join B to the bust point.

Diag 4
Cut the yoke away and cut from the yoke line to within $\frac{1}{8}$'' (3mm) of D and E and the bust point. Fold out the waist dart to open a dart at B, and spread the sections apart at A and C. More fullness should be added at C than at A. Correct the curve of the yoke line.

The back pattern may be made in the same way.

Both these adaptations show a bodice which is tight fitting at the waist, with the entire waist dart transferred to the yoke seam.

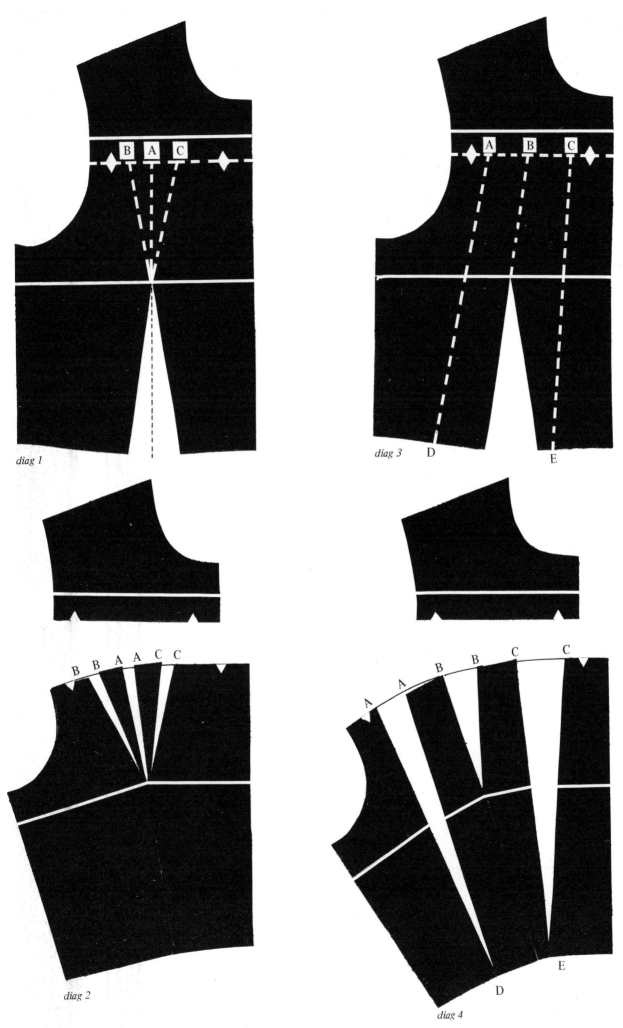

diag 1

diag 3

diag 2

diag 4

29

Yoked styles

If a one-piece dress which is fairly *loose* fitting at the waist is required, the front one-piece block (page 40) should be outlined. Draw the yoke seam, mark balance points and transfer the u/arm dart into the yoke seam (diag 5)). This would only give a very small amount of fullness at the yoke. For greater fullness, the one-piece dress block could be cut along the waist line, the entire waist dart folded out and two further cuts made each side of the bust point, (A and B, diag 6). (Slightly more fullness should be added at B than at A.) The side seam should then be curved from the u/arm point to the hip line, by-passing the side seam of the block. (Ensure that the side seam length, from u/arm point to hip line, is equal to that of the one-piece dress block, disregarding the u/arm dart.)

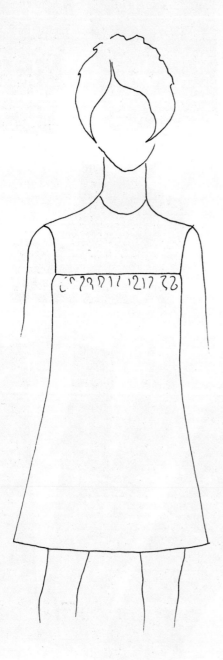

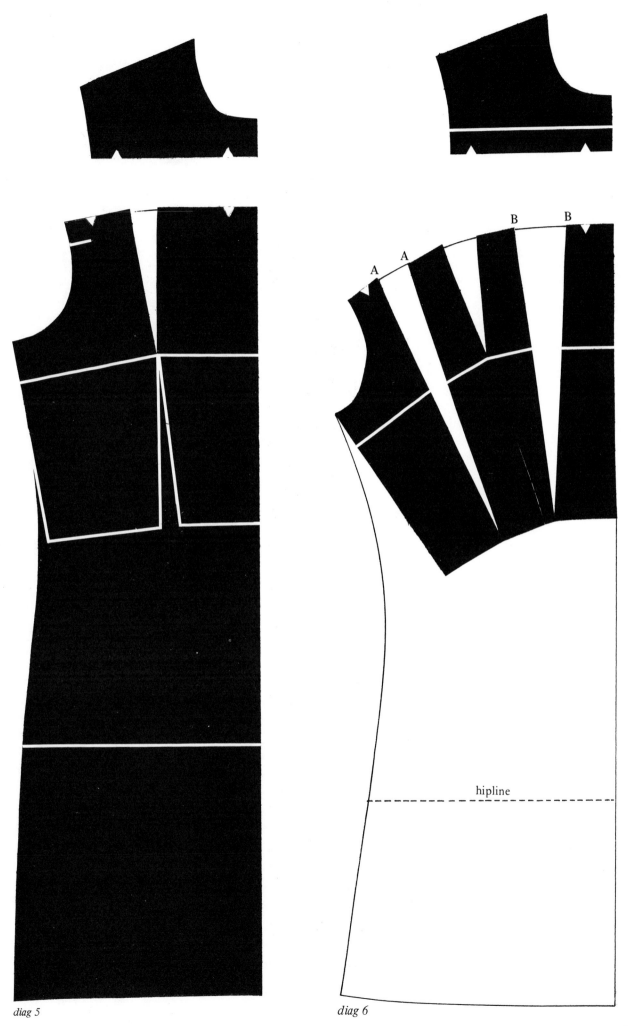

diag 5

diag 6

hipline

A   A   B   B

A   A   B   B

diag 7

32

To make the pattern for a 'smock' dress, adapt the one-piece dress block as shown in diag 5, then make three cuts parallel to the c/f—from the bust point to the hem and from 2'' (5.0cm) each side of the bust point, from the yoke seam to the hem (A and B). Spread the sections apart according to the amount of fullness required but adding slightly less fullness at A than at B. Ensure that the hip line remains a straight line and correct the curve of the yoke seam.

In many of the yoked styles the gathers may extend across the yoke seam from the first balance points, or may be concentrated above the bust point as shown in the first sketch. The latter is, however, advisable for styles in which there is only a small amount of fullness.

smock dress

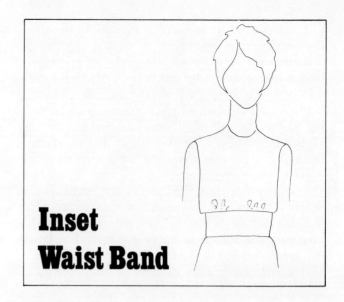

Inset Waist Band

This adaptation is similar in principle to the yoked styles in the previous page, in that a section of the block is cut away and the remaining section is cut and spread apart to privide extra fullness, which is gathered in between the balance marks. As with the yoked styles, the waist dart alone may provide the fullness if only a small amount is required.

Diag 1
Outline the front bodice block. Draw a line above the waist according to the depth of waistband required. The line may be parallel to the waist line or curve to a point at the c/f. Mark balance points as shown. Divide the shoulder into three and mark points A and B. Mark points C and D 1½" (3.8cm) each side of the waist dart. Join A-C and B-D and join the bust point to the centre point of the shoulder seam (E).

Diag 2
Cut the waistband away and fold out the dart. Cut from C and D to within $\frac{1}{8}$" (3mm) of A and B, and from the bust point to within $\frac{1}{8}$" (3mm) of E. Spread the sections apart depending on the amount of fullness required.

Back
Diag 3
Cut the waistband away as for the front and fold out the dart. The pattern may then be cut and spread apart in the same way as at the front, or it may be plain as shown with the remainder of the waist dart sewn as a dart.

The gathers may extend across the c/f and c/b or be concentrated in two groups below the bust point or shoulder blades, as shown in the sketch.

diag 1

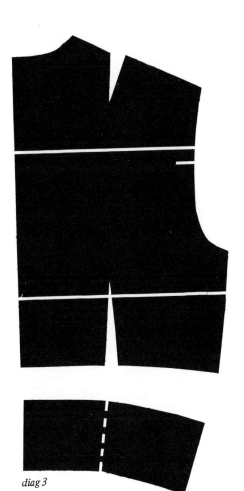

diag 3

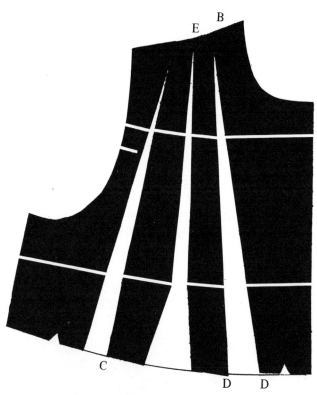

Diag 2

35

Panel Seams

Panel seams are vertical seams in a bodice which pass over, or close to, the bust point or shoulder blades. A panel seam may curve from the a/h (diags 1, 2 and 3), the shoulder (diags 4, 5, 6 and 7) or the neckline, and serves the same purpose as a dart since part of the waist dart is transferred into it. Panel seams are used in tailored garments since they fit more smoothly than darts, due to the fact that they pass over most of the main curves of the body and thus provide shaping where it is most needed. However, a panel seam which passes directly over the bust point is very conspicuous and the panel seam may sometimes be combined with a dart so that the seam is moved further towards the side of the figure (diags 8 and 9).

Panel seam from a/h (diags 1, 2 and 3)
Front
This is the classical type of panel seam, also known as the Princess line.

Draw the centre line of the waist dart and curve the panel line from the bust point to the a/h—usually to the balance point (diag 1). It is important that the panel seam curves smoothly into the centre line of the dart. Mark balance points and cut along the panel line. (Balance points are essential in all panel seams to ensure that the curved sections are correctly joined.) Correct the curve of the side panel around the bust point (it will be slightly pointed due to the waist dart) and draw the straight grain line at right angles to the waist line. Correct the line of the centre panel by adding approx ½" (13mm) at the waist (A) and joining to the bust point (diag 2). This amount may be subtracted from the side panel as shown by the broken line if the bodice is required to fit very closely at the waist.

Back (diag 3)
Draw the centre line of the dart and curve the panel line to the balance point on the a/h or slightly above it. Mark balance points and cut along the panel line. Correct the curve of the side panel if necessary and draw the straight grain line on the side panel at right angles to the waist.

See page 42 for the adaptation of the one-piece dress to a panel seamed bodice (Princess line).

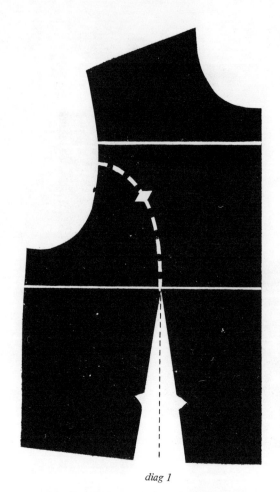

diag 1

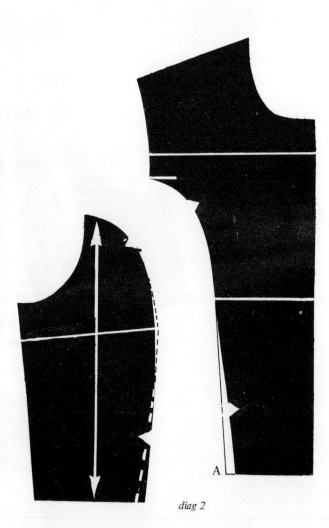

A

diag 2

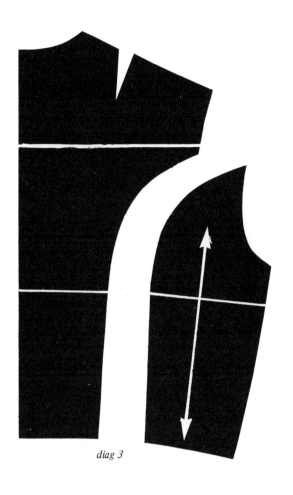

diag 3

Panel seam from Shoulder (diags 4, 5, 6 and 7)
Front
Draw the centre line of the waist dart and draw
the panel line in the required position—usually
from the centre point of the shoulder seam or
slightly nearer the neck—curving smoothly to the
bust point (diag 4). Mark balance points and draw
the straight grain line on the side panel, at right
angles to the waist line. Cut along the panel line
and curve the side panel smoothly over the bust
point. Straighten the line of the centre panel by
adding approximately ½" (13mm) at the waist
line and joining to the bust point. This amount
may be subtracted from the side panel (as shown
by the broken line) if the bodice is required to fit
very closely at the waist (diag 5).

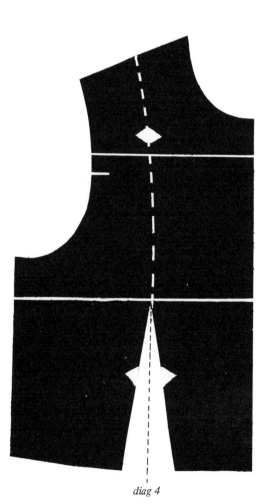

diag 4

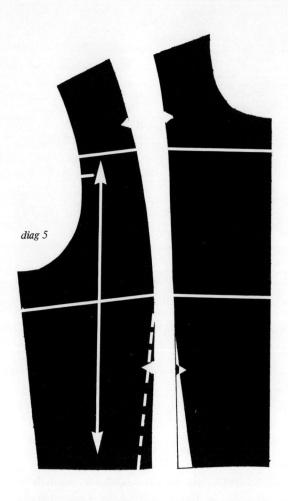

diag 5

panel line by placing the shoulder seams together. Move the shoulder dart, if necessary, until the right hand edge coincides with the panel line. Make balance marks as shown and cut along the panel line. Trim the shoulder dart away, curving it smoothly into the panel line. Draw the straight grain line on the side panel at right angles to the waistline.

The method for making a one-piece dress pattern with shoulder panel seams is the same as that for the Princess dress—page 42.

Back (diags 6 and 7)

Outline the back bodice block and draw the centre line of the waist dart. Draw the panel line from the point of the waist dart to the shoulder, ensuring that it curves smoothly into the front

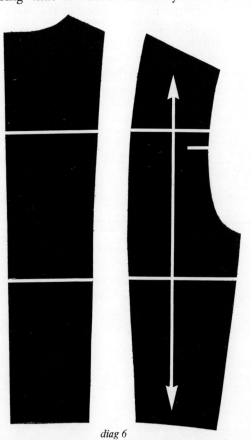

diag 6

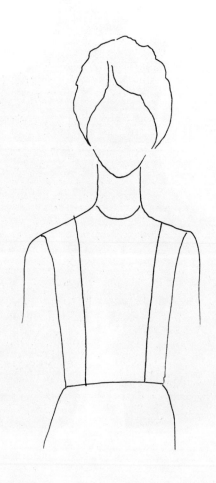

Panel seam with dart

Draw the panel seam from a point approximately mid-way between the side seam and the balance point, curving to meet the waistline at right angles, as shown. The curve should pass 2"-4" (5.0cm-10.2cm) from the bust point. Draw the dart line from approximately ½" (13mm) below the bust line to the bust point (diag 8). Make balance marks and cut along the panel line. Draw the straight grain line on the side panel at right angles to the waistline. Cut along the dart line and transfer part of the waist dart into it. (In some fabrics it may be possible for the dart to be eased in instead of sewn as a dart.)

Diag 3 would be used for the back pattern.

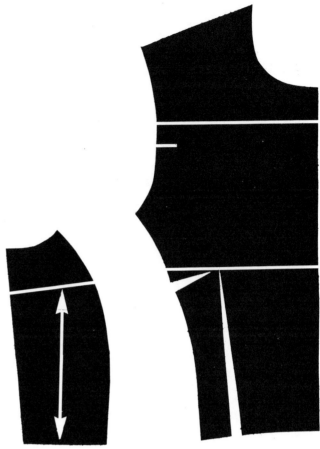

diag 8

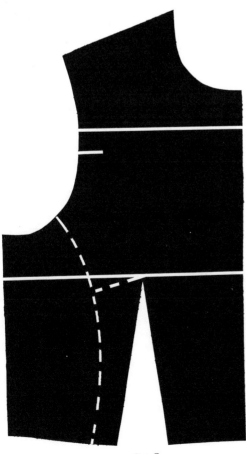

diag 7

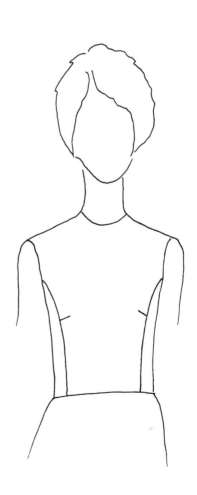

One Piece Dress

A one-piece dress is a dress in which there are no horizontal seams, i.e. at waist, hip or bust. There are usually only five seams altogether—at the shoulders and sides and c.b. The dress has a slightly flared skirt, 4" (10.2cm) wider at the hem

than the skirt block, and is fitted at the waist, allowing only 2"-3" (5.0cm-7.6cm)ease. (For a 'shift' type of dress the waist darts would be omitted or very much reduced.) The one-piece dress provides a useful pattern from which to adapt other styles.

Back
Outline the back bodice block. Continue the c/b line downwards for the length required (A-B). Place the back skirt block with the c/b against the line A-B and with bodice and skirt waist lines together at A. (The waistlines will overlap at the side seams.) Outline the skirt block, disregarding the waist line and dart.

Side seam
Add 1" (2.5cm) extra width at the hem and join to just above the hip line (C). Curve the side seam from C into the bodice side seam as shown, bypassing the waistline.

Waist dart
Extend the centre line of the bodice dart to 6" (15.3cm) below the waistline (D). Join D to the dart edges. The edges of the dart should be curved so that bodice and skirt darts join smoothly, avoiding a point at the waist, as shown by the broken lines on the bodice. The dart may be made narrower or omitted altogether, if a very loose fitting dress is required.

Front
Outline the front bodice block and transfer approximately half of the waist dart into an u/arm dart, as shown. Continue the c/f line downwards for the length required (E-F). Measure the amount of overlap between back bodice and skirt blocks at the side waist. Place the front skirt block to the bodice with the same amount of overlap at the side and with the c/f against the line E-F. (There will be a gap of approximately ½" (13mm) at the c/f waist.) Outline the skirt block, disregarding the waist line and dart.

Side seam
Add 1" (2.5cm) extra width at the hem and join to just above the hip line (G).
    Place the back dress pattern face downwards on the front pattern with points C and G together and the back side seam touching the front seam at the lower point of the u/arm dart (H). Trace the curve. This is the easiest way to ensure that the curves are identical.

Waist dart
Square down from the bust point to 4"-5" (10.2cm-12.7cm) below the waistline (J). Make a 1" (2.5cm) wide dart (or as required), curving to J and to 2" (5.0cm) below the bust point. Also shorten the u/arm dart to 2" (5.0cm) from the bust point. The dart may be narrowed or omitted if desired, as far as the back waist dart.

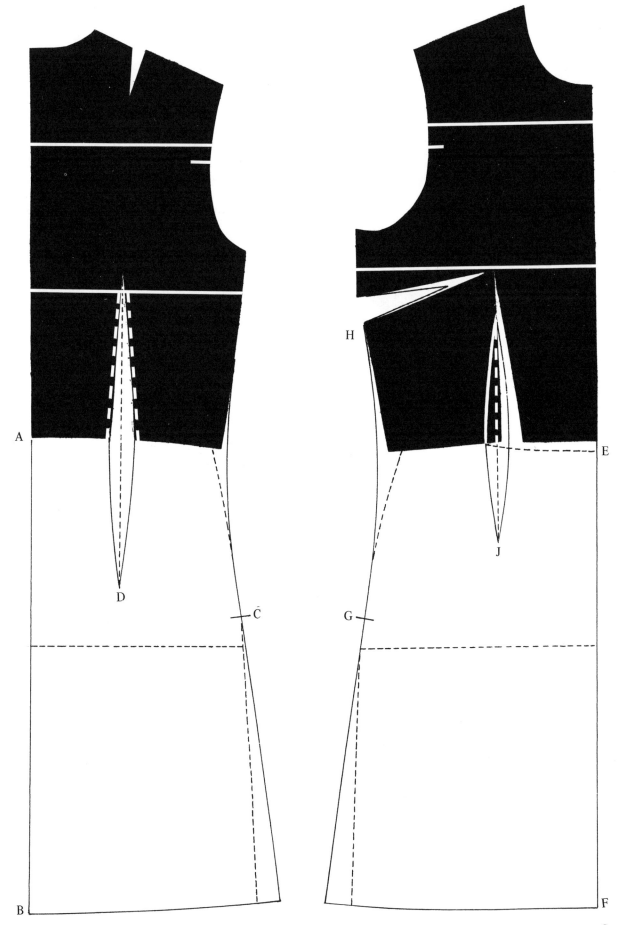

Princess Line Dress

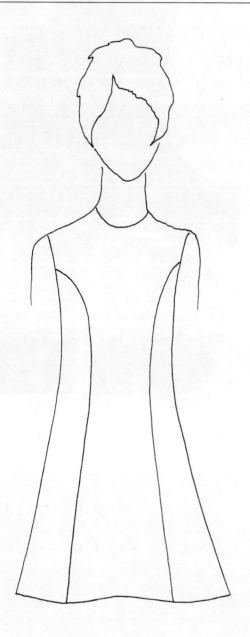

Outline the back one-piece dress (page 40). Continue the centre line of the waist dart to the hem (A) and mark a point on that line 2" (5.0cm) above the hip line (B). Curve from the upper point of the waist dart (C) to the a/h, meeting it in the region of the back width line (D). The line A-B-C-D is the basic panel line, without waist shaping or hem flare.

Add 1"-2" (2.5cm-5.0cm) flare to each panel at the hem (E and F) and join E-B and F-B. Continue each line above B for 3"-4" (7.6cm-10.2cm) as a guide, then curve along the sides of the waist dart to C, and into the panel line. (It is often necessary to take the curve slightly to one side of the panel line below C, as shown in diag 1, in order to draw a good curve on both panels.) Draw the straight grain line on the side panel parallel to the c/b. The c/b seam may also be shaped, as shown in diag 1, if required. Measure out approx. 1" (2.5cm) at the hem (G) and join to H 2" (5.0cm) above the hip line. Continue the line towards the waist, then curve to approx. ½" (13mm) from the c/b at the waist line and into the c/b at the bust line.

Cut along the line F-B-C-D to obtain the centre panel, then trace the side panel. Add the hem flare (i.e. the distance between E and F) and cut away the waist dart. Diag 2 page 44 shows the completed patterns.

Front—diags 3 & 4
Outline the front *bodice* block and adapt it to a panel seamed bodice as shown on page 36. Adapt the panel seamed bodice to a one-piece dress as shown on page 40.

The front pattern is then made in exactly the same way as the back, except that the panel line curves into the sides of the dart at the a/h (G and H), instead of into a single point (diag 2). Diag 4 shows the completed pattern.

The small amount of additional ease on the hip line which is caused by joining the panel lines to a point 2" (5.0cm) above the hip line, is to counteract the tightening effect of the extra layers of fabric caused by panel seams.

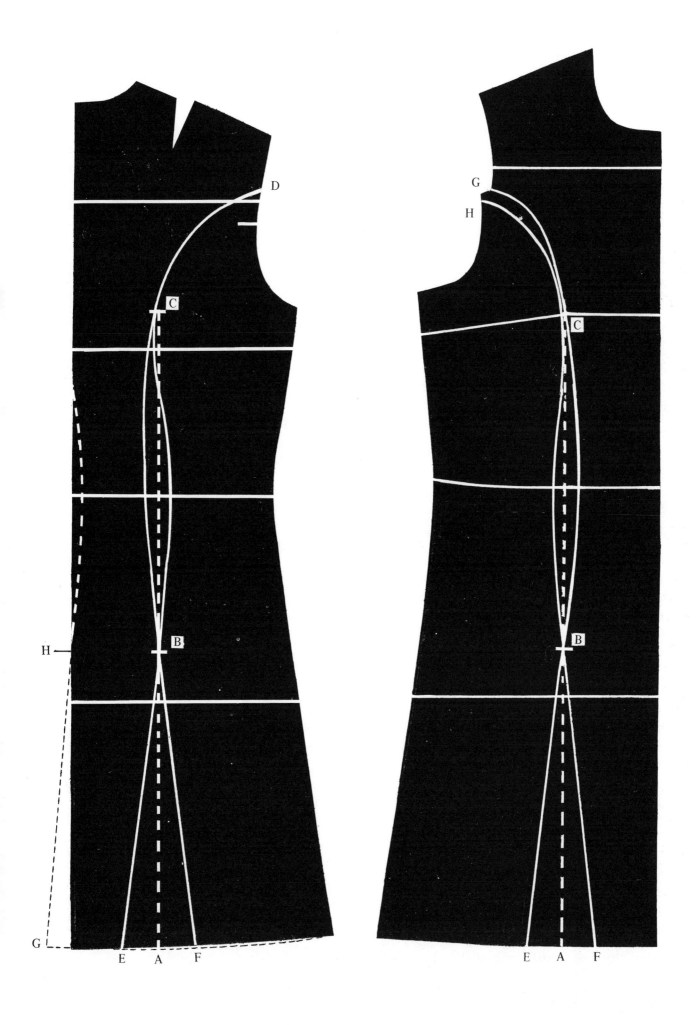

diag 1

diag 3

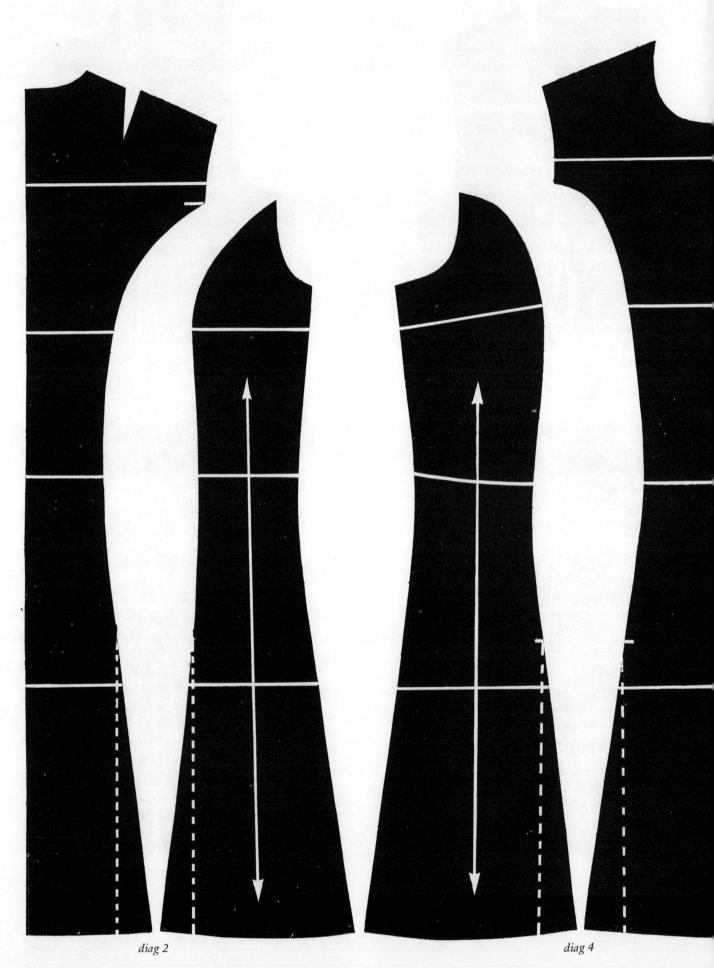

diag 2

diag 4

Low Neckline

It is always advisable to tighten the neckline of a low-necked style to avoid 'gaping'.

When drawing a new neckline on a pattern, place the front and back patterns together at the shoulder seam and draw the complete neckline, from c/f to c/b. This ensures that the curve of the neckline is continuous across the shoulder seam. If the back neckline is also to be cut down it should be tightened in the same way as shown for the front—by transferring fullness into the waist dart (which must be extended approximately 2'' (5.0cm) to reach the shoulder blades). The dart may be sewn in the neckline of the dress but folding out the dart in the pattern is neater and generally preferable.

N.B. It is very important that these adaptations, and that on the following page, are made *after* the waist dart, or part of it, has been transferred to the required position. The neckline dart is then transferred into the remaining part of the waist dart as shown in the diags.

Square neckline (diags 1 and 2)
Outline the front bodice block and draw the neckline in the required position. The horizontal line must be at right angles to the c/f and is usually straight; the side edge may be curved or straight and is usually slanted. Ensure that the back and front necklines join smoothly at the shoulder seam. Cut along the new neckline. Draw a dart from the bust point to the neckline in the position shown, making the dart ½''-1'' (13mm-2.5cm) wide. Fold out (see page 26) the dart, transferring it into the *waist* dart, not the u/arm dart to obtain the shape shown in diag 2. Correct the shape of the neckline at point A. The waist dart is now wider because the neckline dart has been transferred into it but the excess width may be disregarded when making a one-piece dress pattern (page 40).

Scooped neckline (diags 3 and 4)
Outline the front and back bodice blocks and draw the neckline in the required position, ensuring that there is a right angle between the curve and the c/f. Cut along the new neckline. Draw a dart from the bust point to the neckline in the position shown, making the dart ½''-1'' (13mm-2.5cm) wide. Fold out the dart, transferring it into the waist dart to obtain the shape in diag 4. Correct the curve of the neckline.

'V' neckline (diags 5 and 6)
Outline the front and back bodice blocks and draw the neckline in the required position,

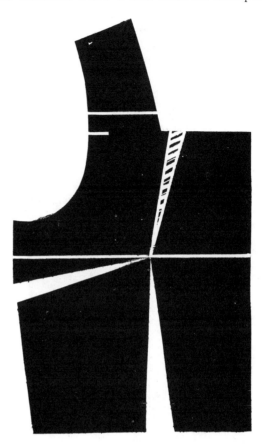

diag 1

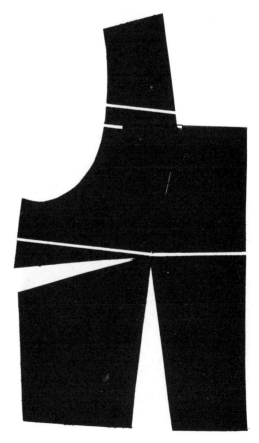

diag 2

the position shown and fold out the dart,
transferring it into the waist dart, to obtain the
shape in diag 6. Correct the shape of the neckline,
as shown.

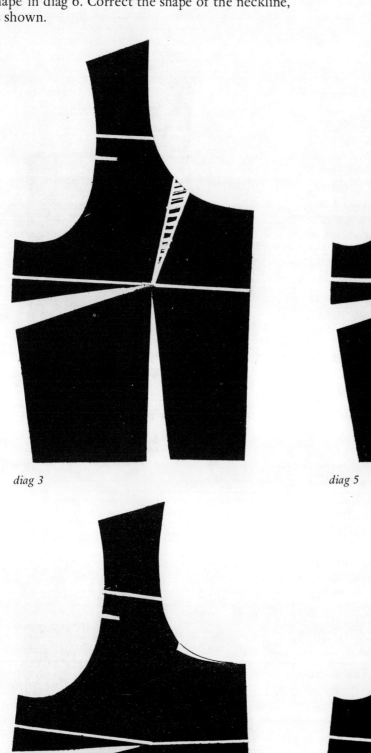

diag 3

diag 5

diag 4

diag 6

Sleeveless Styles

The bodice blocks shown on page 10 are intended for a dress with sleeves and therefore *must* be adapted for sleeveless styles. A dress without sleeves needs a slightly higher, closer-fitting a/h than one with sleeves and so the depth and the length around the a/h must be reduced. The upper part of the a/h usually fits satisfactorily and the size of the a/h should therefore be reduced in the lower part.

Outline the front bodice block. Raise the u/arm point ½" (13mm) and curve smoothly into the original line as shown in diag 1. Draw a dart from the bust point to the a/h in the position shown, making the dart ¾"-1¼" (19mm-3.1cm) wide. The exact amount needed for each individual figure can only be found by experiment. Fold out the dart to obtain the shape in diag 2 and correct the curve of the a/h. Adapt the back pattern in the same way (diags 3 and 4)—raise the u/arm point ½" (13mm) and draw a dart from the a/h to the point of the waist dart, but make the dart approximately half the width needed at the front. Transfer the dart into the waist dart and correct the curve of the a/h.

The front width, back width and shoulder may each be narrowed ¼" (6mm) if desired.

N.B. It is very important that this adaptation, and those on the previous page, are made *after* the waist dart, or part of it, has been transferred to the required position. The a/h dart is then folded out into the remaining part of the waist dart, as shown in the diagrams.

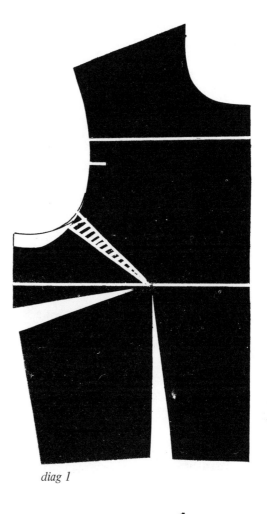

diag 1

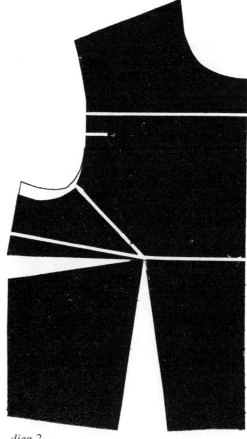

diag 2

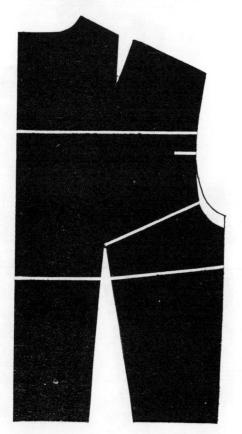

diag 3

diag 4

Coat Blocks

The bodice blocks on page 10 are intended to make a dress or blouse pattern and must be adapted to incorporate more ease before they can be used for any garment which is to be worn over another, such as a coat or jacket. This involves increasing the ease allowance on the bust and hip lines by at least 2'' (5.0cm), thus making the total ease allowance at least 4'' (10.2cm), and making proportionate increases in other areas. The a/hs are made slightly deeper to allow a dress to be accommodated underneath. The blocks should also be made larger for a pinafore dress or for the type of s/less jacket shown on page 57 but less ease is needed than for a coat and the amounts shown here should be *halved*. The a/hs may be made deeper, or not, according to preference but must be tightened as shown on page 47.

Back

Outline the back bodice block. Raise the shoulder point and neck point ¼'' (6mm) and draw the new shoulder seam parallel to the original. (Raising the neck and shoulder points gives extra ease in the shoulder area to allow for interfacing and lining.) Make the shoulder dart the same width as in the original seam. Lower the neckline $\frac{1}{8}$'' (3mm) all round. Widen the shoulder by ¼'' (6mm) and the back width ¼''-½'' (3mm-6mm) (according to the amount of ease preferred across the back) and deepen the a/h by ½'' (13mm). Draw the new a/h as shown. Add ¼'' (6mm) to the side seam and curve the new line parallel to the original. A fitted coat or jacket often has a curved seam to enable the waist to fit closely, but this is optional and in a loose-fitting coat may be omitted. Mark a point ½''-¾'' (13mm-19mm) from the c/b on the waist line and curve into the straight c/b just above the bust line. (Avoid reducing the width on the bustline more than necessary when curving this line.)

Front

Raise the neck and shoulder points ¼'' (6mm) and draw the new shoulder seam. Lower the neckline $\frac{1}{8}$'' (3mm) all round. Draw the new c/f line ½'' (13mm) from the original. (This addition counteracts the tendency of the front edges to part when the coat is worn unbuttoned and allows more ease over the bust.) Although the front neckline is widened by this addition, the back neckline remains the same so that the coat neckline will fit closely at the side of the neck. Widen the shoulder ¼'' (6mm) but do not increase the front width since ½'' (13mm) has been added to this m/ment at the c/f. Deepen the

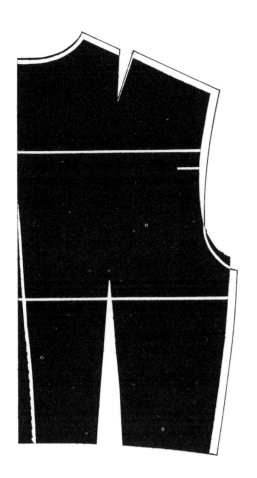

a/h ½" (13mm) and draw the new a/h as shown. Add ¼" (6mm) to the side seam.

Unless the coat is to fit edge-to-edge the pattern must have an allowance added to the d/f for an overlap (see page 52). As stated on page 52, the overlap would be 1½"-3"(3.8cm-7.6cm) for a single breasted coat and 4"-8" (10.2cm-20.4cm) for a double breasted coat. Half the required amount should be added to the c/f. Whenever possible, the facing should also be cut in one piece with the front of the coat, as shown on page 52 for a blouse. If the coat is to have a turned back lapel (rever) draw the roll line (the line along which the lapel turns back) on the pattern, mark the required depth of the opening on the c/f (A) and join to a point approx ½" (13mm) out from the neck point (B). Point B always remains approximately in that position regardless of the slant of the roll line.

The amounts added to the pattern allow 2" (5.0cm) extra ease on the bust line (4" (10.2cm) altogether) but if more ease is required ½"-¾" (13mm-19mm) may be added to the side seams, instead of ¼" (6mm), and $\frac{5}{8}$,"-¾" (16mm-19mm) to the c/f instead of ½" (13mm). If the maximum amounts were added, the total ease would be 6½" (16.5cm).

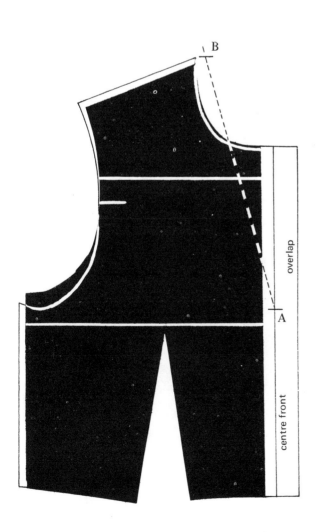

Sleeve

The sleeve block must be increased in width across the top arm line by 1½"-2" (3.8cm-5.00cm) to allow for a dress to be worn underneath and to enable it to fit the larger a/h of the coat.

Outline the sleeve block and make the s/h ½" (13mm) deeper (by lowering the u/arm line) to correspond with the deeper a/h. Cut through the front arm and back arm lines and add ½" (13mm) at each. This ensures that the s/h is widened in addition to the top arm line. Add ¼"-½" (6mm-13mm) to each side seam. The amount added will depend on the length around the a/hs of the coat block, which should be 1"-2" (2.5cm-5.0cm) less than the m/ment around the s/h.

The coat sleeve block would then probably, although not necessarily, be adapted to a two-piece sleeve as shown on page 121. The one-piece semi-fitted sleeve on page 97 may be preferred for some coats, especially those which are loose fitting.

Having adapted the bodice and sleeve blocks as shown, a coat pattern is made by adapting the coat blocks to the style required exactly in the same way as for a dress pattern: step-by-step according to the method of work on page 20. For instance, a Princess style coat pattern is made according to the dress method shown on page 42 and may use the Princess style bodice with panel seam from the a/h (as shown), the Princess bodice with dart (page 38) or the shoulder panelled bodice (page 37); or a looser fitting coat may be made according to the one-piece dress adaptation (page 40), having first moved part of the front waist dart to the required position.

For this reason it is not necessary to adapt the skirt blocks providing it is remembered that the ease allowed on the hip line of a coat must be at least 4" (10.2cm).

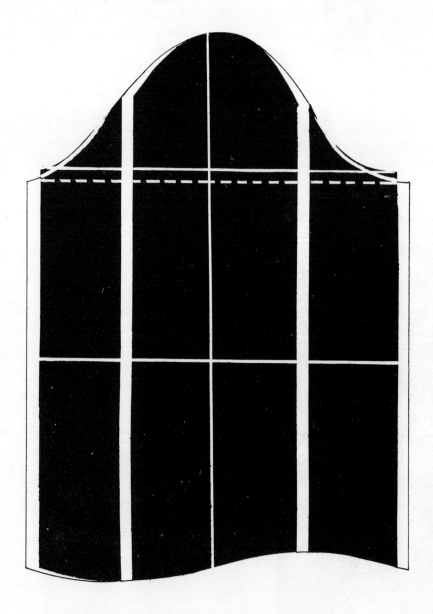

Openings and Facings

Shirt
Rever
Shaped rever
Fly front
Tunic shirt
Waistcoat

Openings

Shirt

A bodice which has an opening with buttons and buttonholes at the c/f (or c/b) must have an allowance added to the c/f to enable the front edges to overlap.

The amount added to the c/f for the overlap is half of the total overlap required, since the pattern represents only half of the bodice. The usual total overlap for a blouse or dress is ¾"-1½" (19mm-3.8cm) and for a coat or jacket 1½"-3" (3.8cm-7.6cm), unless it is a double breasted style in which case the overlap would be 4"-8" (10.2cm-20.5cm).

The front edge must also have a facing added which folds under to neaten and strengthen the front edge. The facing may sometimes have to be cut as a separate pattern piece (page 54 diag 4) but should be cut in one piece with the bodice whenever possible.

The width of the facing for a blouse or dress should not be less than 3" (7.6cm) and for a coat not less than 4" (10.2cm).

Diag 1

This opening is only suitable if the bodice is to remain closed at the neckline, e.g. with a shirt collar or Peter Pan collar.

Add half the total overlap required to the c/f and draw the front edge (broken line). Add the width of facing required to the front edge. Fold the pattern along the front edge and trace the curve of the neckline. This is very important as otherwise the edge of the facing cannot be supported in the neckline seam.

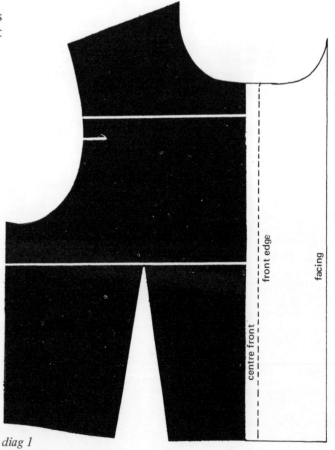

diag 1

Rever

Diag 2

This opening is suitable for a bodice which opens at the neck, e.g. with a collar and rever. Add half the total overlap required to the c/f and draw the front edge (broken line). Fold the pattern along the front edge and trace the neckline curve and part of the shoulder seam. Make the facing at least 3" (7.6cm) wide at the hem and at least 2" (5.0cm) wide at the shoulder. Curve the outer edge of the facing as shown.

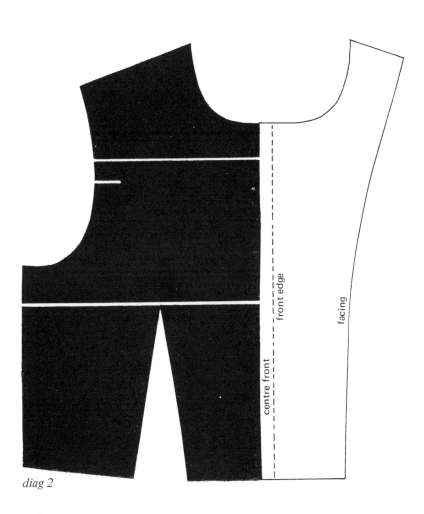

diag 2

Shaped Rever

Diags 3 and 4
This facing is used with wide revers which extend beyond the front edge. Add half the required width of overlap and draw a line parallel to the c/f (line A-B).

Mark the depth of opening required on the c/f (C). Draw the roll line (the line along which the rever folds back) from a point approximately ½" (13mm) from the neck point (D) passing through C and extending to the front edge (E). Fold the rever back along the roll line and draw the rever in the required shape, ensuring that it curves smoothly into the front edge at E. Draw the facing line (broken white line) according to the width of facing required. Unlike the two previous methods, in which the front edge is straight thus enabling the facing to be cut in one piece with the bodice, this adaptation requires a separate facing.

Trace the facing section as shown in diag 4.

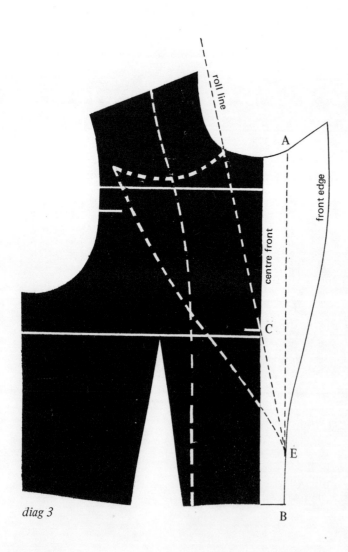

diag 3

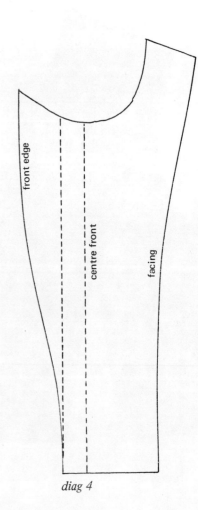

diag 4

Fly Front

Diag 5

This method enables both the buttons and the stitching to be hidden but requires a large amount of material. In the diagram, the broken line A-B is the centre line of the finished opening, the broken lines C-D and E-F are the *inward* folds and the solid lines G-H, J-K and L-M are the *outward* folds. The lines C-D and E-F are sewn together to make the box pleat which conceals stitching and buttons.

Assuming the finished band to be 2" (5.0cm) wide:

Section 1 should be 1" (2.5cm) wide, section 2 (being the width of the finished band) should be 2" (5.0cm) wide, section 3 should be 1" (2.5cm) wide, section 4 should be ¾" (19mm) wide and section 5, the facing, should be approximately 3" (7.6cm) wide. (Section 4 is made ¼" (6mm) narrower than section 3 to prevent the under fold showing.)

This opening should be practised by making paper folds before it is attempted in fabric.

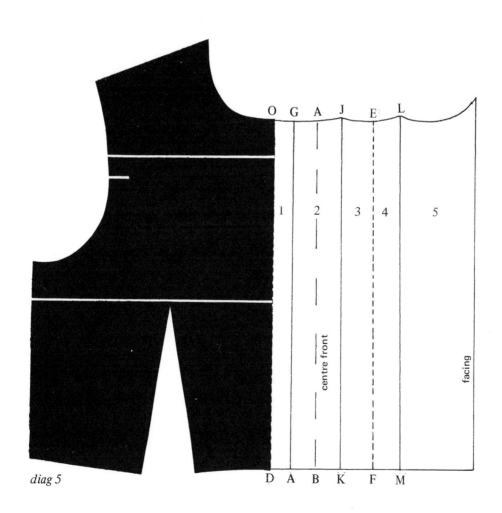

diag 5

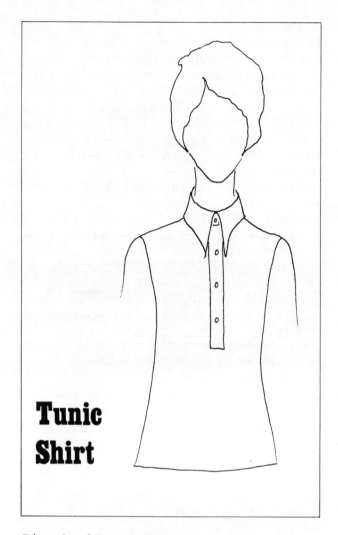

Tunic Shirt

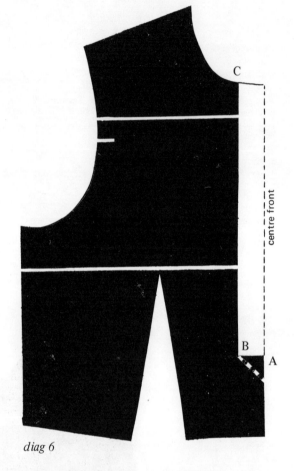

diag 6

Diags 6 and 7

This opening has a band set in at the c/f which extends to just above waist level.

Mark the depth of opening required on the c/f (A). Square across from A for half the width of band required (B) and draw a line from B to the neckline (C), parallel to the c/f. Cut away the rectangle A-B-C.

The band should measure the length of the opening (B-C) by four times A-B, half of which is the extension and half is the facing as shown in diag 2. Curve the top edge of the band and facing according to the curve of the neckline.

A point or curve may be added to the extension as shown if required.

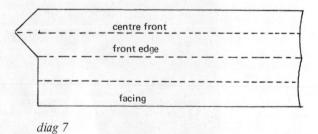

diag 7

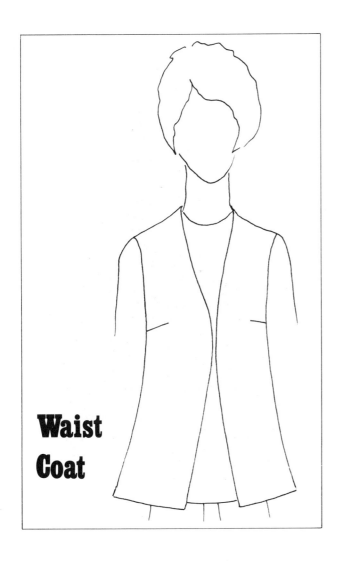

Waist Coat

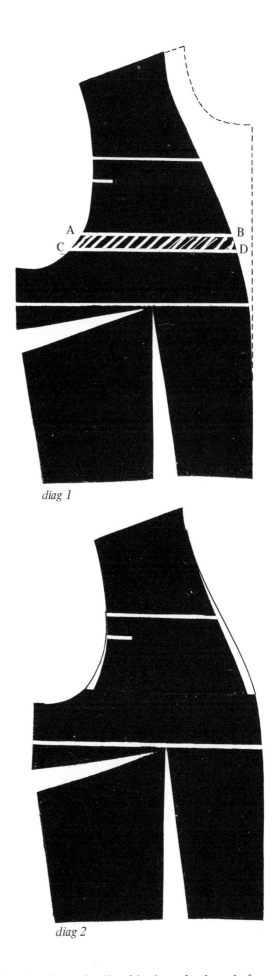

diag 1

diag 2

It is usually necessary to shorten the centre front length of an edge-to-edge jacket pattern, due to the tendency of the corners of the hemline to drop and thus hang apart (see sketch).

If the jacket is s/less the pattern would need to be tightened at the a/h in addition to the neckline, and this can most easily be accomplished by folding a pleat across the pattern as shown in diags 1 and 2.

Outline the front bodice block and adapt it for a jacket as described on page 49. Draw the neckline in the required position and draw the straight grain line parallel to the c/f. Cut along the neckline. Transfer part of the waist dart into an u/arm dart, or as required. Draw a line across parallel to the front width line and approx 3" (7.6cm) below it (A-B). Draw the line C-D ½" (13mm) below A-B (diag 1) and the amount between the two lines is then folded out to obtain the shape in diag 2. Correct the curves of a/h and neckline carefully.

The a/h of the back pattern should be tightened as shown on page 47 and front and back patterns extended below the waist according to the instructions for a one-piece dress as shown on page 40. The facing pattern for the front edge should be made as shown on page 54, diag 4.

If the jacket is to have sleeves it is only necessary to tighten the neckline as shown in diags 3 and 4.

Outline the front bodice block and adapt it for a jacket as described on page 49. Draw the new neckline in the required position and draw the straight grain line parallel to the c/f. Cut along the neckline. Transfer part of the waist dart into an u/arm dart, or as required. Measure up ½" (13mm) from the bust line (A) and join to the bust point to form a dart. (Diag 3) Fold out the dart, transferring it into the *waist* dart to obtain the shape shown in diag 4. Correct the curve of the neckline and correct the straight grain line by continuing the lower part upwards. The back pattern would need to be adapted as shown on page 49 and extended below the waist as shown on page 40 for a one-piece dress, as would the front pattern. The facing pattern for the front edge should be made as shown on page 54, diag 4.

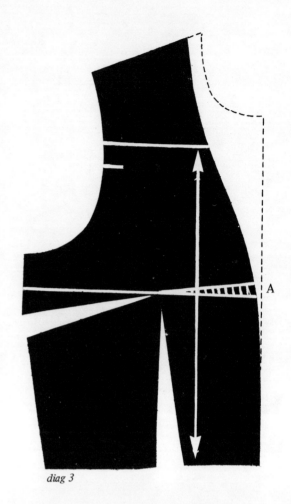

diag 3

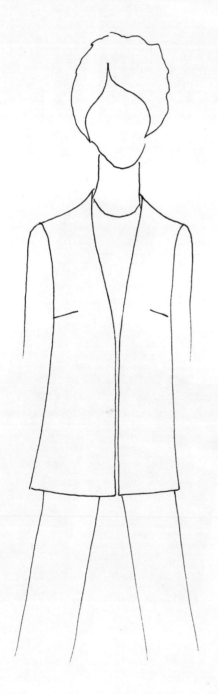

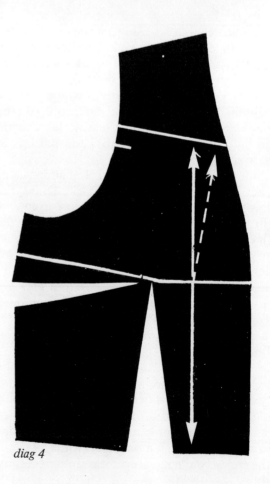

diag 4

Capes

Basic cape
Narrow cape
Semi circular cape
Circular cape

Capes

Basic Cape

A cape is essentially a loose fitting garment and is most flattering and attractive when it is sufficiently full to enable it to fall in soft folds. The patterns for full capes must be developed from the basic cape pattern (page 61) to ensure that the fullness falls evenly around the figure and is not concentrated at the sides.

The minimum hem width for a successful cape is approximately 80" (230cm)—this cape would have an 'A' shaped silhouette but would have very little fullness (see sketch on page 62).

N.B. All hem widths given are related to a 36" (91.5cm) centre front length.

(All other cape patterns are developed from this pattern). The shoulder seam *must* be centralised before making a cape pattern—it may even be advisable to bring the seam forward a further ½" (13 mm) to counteract the tendency of a cape to slip back off the shoulders.

Outline the front and back bodice blocks. Centralise the shoulder seam and adapt the blocks to coat blocks as shown on page 49. (In practice, only the neckline and shoulder adaptations need be made since the cape pattern is not affected by the shape of the a/h or side seam.) Cut out the blocks. (In diag 1 the black shapes represent the bodice blocks with the above adjustments made.)

Place the front block close to the right hand side of the paper leaving a margin of approximately 12" (30.5cm) above it. Extend the c/f line above the neckline for 10" (25.4cm) and mark point A. Square out 12" (30.5cm) from point A and mark point B. From B draw a line at 45° to A-B (line B-C). Place the back block with shoulder point (D) 1" (2.5cm) from the front shoulder point (E) and c/b line parallel to the line B-C.

Extend the c/f line downwards and measure the required length from the neckline. Mark point F at the hem. Extend the c/b line downwards and mark the length, (G) which should be 2" (5.0cm) longer than at the c/f. Square out short guide lines from F and G, as shown.

Mark the overarm line by folding the pattern in half with c/f and c/b together and creasing it along the fold. (Ensure that the overarm line passes mid-way between points D and E.) Measure 4" (10.2cm) along the overarm line from the shoulder points and mark point H. Curve from H into the front and back shoulder seams, bypassing D and E by approximately ¼" (6mm). These curves form the shoulder dart and it is essential that the dart is continued below the shoulder point to ensure that the cape curves smoothly over the shoulder. However, due to the extreme width of the dart, it is often better to cut this cape in two parts, with a seam along the overarm line, as shown in diags 2 and 3. The side length should be approx 5" (12.7cm) longer than the c/f to allow for the curve over the shoulder bone. Measure from the front neck point (J) along the shoulder curve to H, then along the overarm line. Mark point K at the hem. Curve the hemline G-K-F, following each of the guide lines for approx 4" (10.2cm).

To mark the position of the slit—measure one-third of the front hem width (i.e. one-third of K-F) from the c/f (L) and join to J. From E measure the sleeve length of the figure on to the line J-L and mark point M. Measure 6" (15.2cm) up and 4" (10.2cm) down from M to mark the ends of the slit. (Although a slit is easier to use and less likely to tear if it is slanted, it may be made vertical if preferred, for instance to make it less conspicuous in striped or checked fabric.)

The cape may be left plain, with only overarm seams or even with no seams at all, or it may have style seams added. A seam is often made at the front to incorporate the slits as they are then less likely to tear. Unless the cape is to meet edge-to-edge, an allowance must be added to the c/f for an overlap as for a coat (see page 52). The facing should also be added if the fabric is sufficiently wide to allow cape and facing to be cut in one piece (see page 52). A collar or a hood may be added to the neckline.

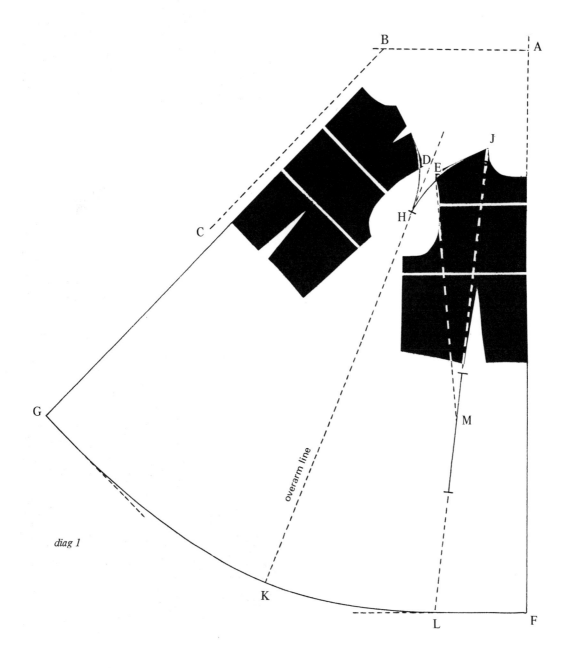

diag 1

Narrow Cape

(Diags 2 and 3)

This cape would have a hem width of approx 80"
(230cm) which is the minimum recommended.
Only the hem width is reduced—the basic cape
must not be made narrower around the shoulders
or it will become too tight to allow the arms to be
raised comfortably.

Adapt the blocks to the basic cape as shown on
the previous page and cut along the overarm line
to obtain the two shapes shown in diagrams 2 and
3. The hem width may be reduced by up to 3"
(7.6cm) on front and back; mark the new hem
points (N) and join to the bust level (P)' Curve
smoothly into the shoulder.

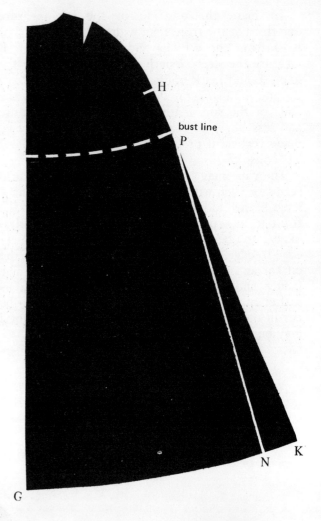

diag 2

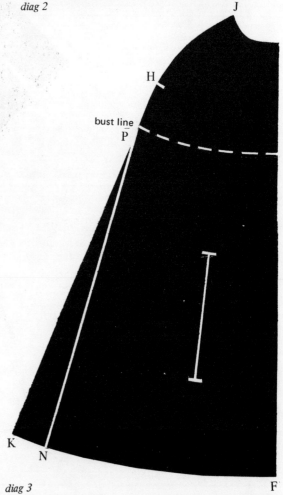

diag 3

Semi Circular Cape

This cape has a hem width of approx 150" (381cm).

Make the basic cape pattern as shown on page 60 but do not mark the slit and cut along the overarm line to obtain the shapes in diags 2 and 3.

Back
Divide the hemline into four equal parts and mark points Q, R and S. Join Q to the centre point of the neckline, R to the point of the shoulder dart and S to the shoulder point. Cut from Q and S to within $\frac{1}{8}$" (3mm) of the edge of the pattern and from R to within $\frac{1}{8}$" (3mm) of the point of the dart. (All sections of the pattern should *just* be held together.)

Spread the sections apart an equal amount at each line until the overarm seam is at an angle of 45° to the c/b, as shown in diag 4. Only a small amount of the shoulder dart remains and this may be eased in when sewing the overarm seam. The straight grain line may be drawn parallel to the c/b or the overarm seam, according to preference.

Front
Make the front pattern in the same way but join the centre of the three lines to the centre point of the shoulder. Mark the position of the slit according to the instructions on page 61.

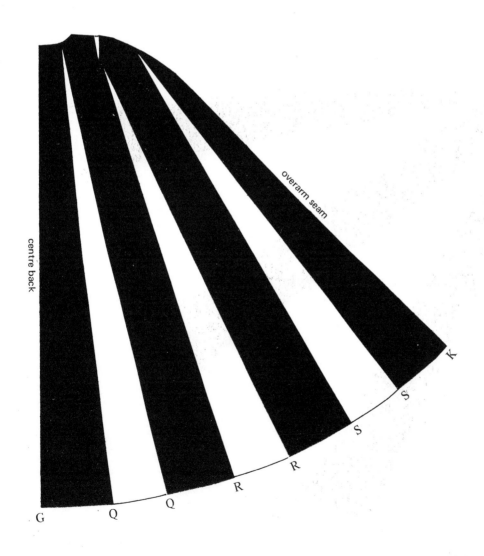

diag 4

The hem width of this cape is approximately 300" (765cm).

Make the pattern as described above for the semi-circular cape but open the sections until the overarm seam is at right angles to the c/b, as shown in diag 5. The shoulder dart is now closed completely. The overarm seam should be a straight line—correct it by squaring across from the neck point (line T-K). Make the front pattern in the same way and mark the slit according to the instructions on page 61. The straight grain line may be drawn parallel to either the c/b or the overarm seam.

Diags 4 and 5 are merely examples of the method of adapting the basic narrow cape—the sections may be spread apart by any amount that is desired, providing that the fullness is evenly distributed.

Circular Cape

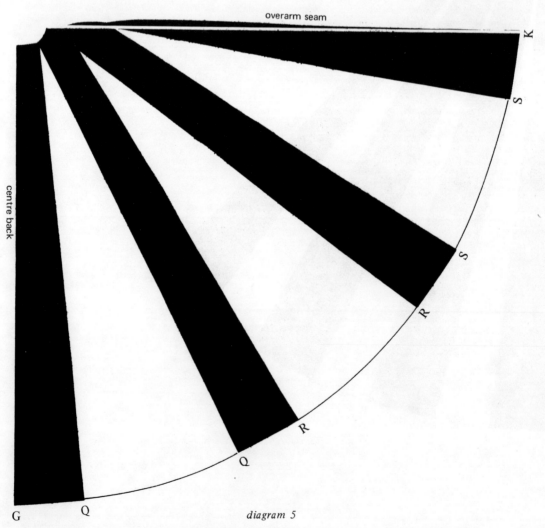

diagram 5

Hoods

Basic pointed
Basic round
Close-fitting round
Draped
Cut in one piece with the bodice

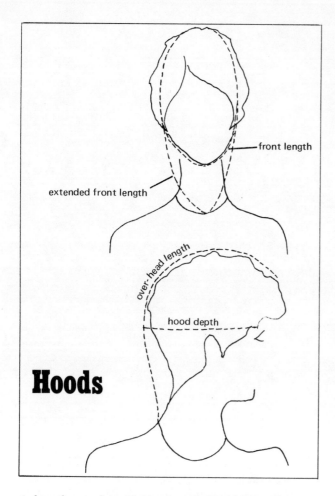

front length

extended front length

over-head length

hood depth

Hoods

Basic Pointed Hood

(Diag 1)

This is a fairly loose fitting hood with 2"-3" (5.0cm-7.6cm) ease around the hood depth line.

Draw a rectangle A-B-C-D measuring half of the front length m/ment (A-B), by half of the hood depth m/ment plus 1"-1½" (2.5cm-3.8cm). (A-D).

Draw the hood depth line as a guide line, approx 6" (15.2cm) below the top line (E-F).

Measure half of the extended length from D along the front edge and mark point G. Join B-G and mark the centre point (H). Curve the neckline from B to G, passing approx ¾" (9mm) above H. Two or three small darts or pleats should be made in the neckline, at right angles to the curve, one to coincide with the shoulder seam and the remainder nearer the c/f, to reduce the hood neckline to that of the bodice.

A hood may be attached to the neckline of a coat or dress or it may be separate and have an extension below the neckline. The shape of a hood depends on the shape of the crown, which may be square, pointed or rounded. A hood may be loose-fitting, shaped to the head or have a lengthened front edge that causes it to drape on the shoulders. Most hood patterns are cut separately from the bodice pattern but one style, which is loose-fitting with a draped front edge, may be cut in one piece with the bodice, (see page 70).

Measurements for hoods
Four m/ments are needed:
    front length
    extended front length
    hood depth
    overhead length
The front length is taken around the side of the face and over the top of the head with the ends of the tape joining under the chin. The extended front length is taken as for the front length but with the ends of the tape meeting at the c/f neckline. The hood depth is measured around the head at eye level and the overhead length is measured from forehead to c/b neckline. (See sketches).

There is very little variation in head sizes but the m/ments may be affected by fashions in hair styling.

All separate hood patterns are developed from two basic patterns—the pointed hood or the round hood.

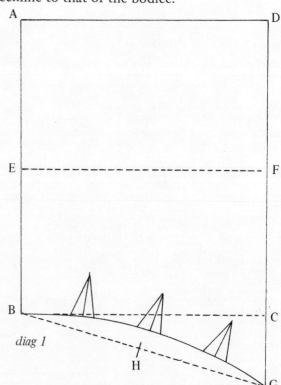

diag 1

Variations on the pointed hood

To give a more exaggerated point to the crown of the hood, point A may be moved approx 1" (2.5cm) upwards and outwards (diag 2).

To make a hood with a squared crown—outline the basic pointed hood and draw a 2" (5.0cm) square at point A (diag 3). The square is cut away and the two sides joined to create the square effect.

Basic Round Hood

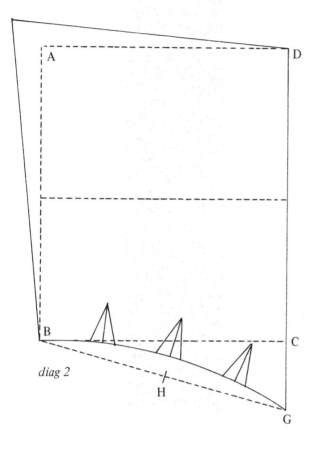

diag 2

(Diag 4)

The round hood is adapted from the basic pointed hood pattern but is made slightly tighter at the front of the head and at the back of the neck. Outline the basic pointed hood pattern and draw a line from A at 45° to A-D. Measure 2" (5.0cm) along this line from A and mark point J. Measure 1" (2.5cm) in from B (K) and ½" (13mm) down from D (L). Curve the overhead seam K-J-L, touching the line A-D and the line A-B as shown. Two darts should be adequate at the neckline since the size of the neckline has already been reduced at K.

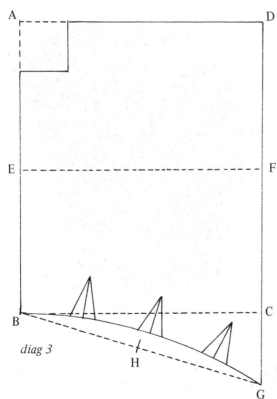

diag 3

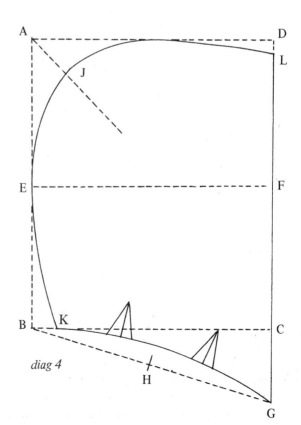

diag 4

Close fitting Round Hood

(Diag 5)

This pattern is shaped by means of a panel set in at the back of the hood and is closer fitting than any of the previous examples.

Outline the basic round hood as shown in diag 4, omitting the darts. Draw a new front edge (M-N) to reduce the line E-F to half of the hood depth m/ment plus ½" (13mm). Raise the neckline curve ½" (13mm) to reduce the front length slightly.

Draw a curve parallel to the curve K-J-L and 2" (5.0cm) from it. (This will give a 4" (10.2cm)

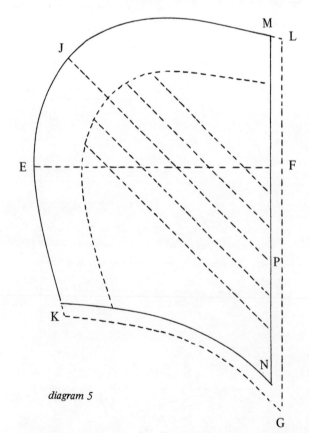

diagram 5

Cut along the curve of the centre panel, measure the *longer* edge (K-J-L) and cut a straight strip that length and 4" (10.2cm) wide (diag 6). Mark the c/b line.

Cut the remaining part of the pattern along the five broken lines from the curve almost to the front edge and open out the sections until the curve measures the same length as the straight

diag 6

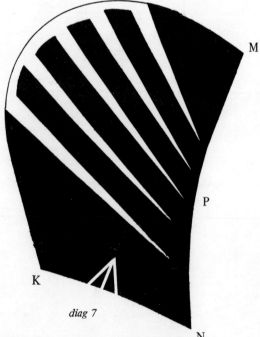

diag 7

wide centre panel.) Extend the line from J to the front edge (P) and draw two lines each side of P as shown, making four 1" (2.5cm) wide sections.

strip (diag 7). Correct the curve. Make one or two darts in the neckline, as required.

N.B. Cut *one* centre panel and *two* side sections.

Draped Hood

Cut in One Piece with the Bodice

Diag 8

The draped hood has a longer front edge which causes it to drape on the shoulders (as shown in the sketch opposite). A draped hood may be pointed, squared or rounded at the crown.

Outline the basic pointed hood and adapt the shape of the crown, if required, or outline the basic round hood. Mark point H 1½" (3.8cm) from B and curve from H to E, continuing the curve to A as shown. Draw a guide line 2"-4" (5.0cm-10.2cm) below G, according to the amount of drape required. From H, measure half of the bodice neckline in a curve on to the guide line and mark point J. Curve the front edge from D, passing approximately ½" (13mm) from F, to J.

Like the draped hood, this pattern has a longer front edge than the basic hoods, which causes it to fall gracefully on the shoulders.

Front—diag 1

Outline the front bodice block and extend the c/f line upwards for 14½" (36.9cm) (A). Mark point B on the shoulder seam 2" (5.0cm) from the neck point and point C 1" (2.5cm) from B. Square up 13" (33cm) from B (i.e. parallel to the extended c/f) and mark point D. Curve the line D-B into the shoulder seam at C, as shown. Mark point E 1" (2.5cm) below the neck point. Square out 1½" (3.8cm) from A (F) and join F-E and F-D.

Back—diag 2

Outline the back bodice block and extend the c/b upwards for approximately 12" (30.5cm). Mark point A 6" (15cm) above the neckline. Mark point B on the shoulder seam 3" (7.6cm) from the neck point and move the shoulder dart along to B as shown. Mark point C 2" (5.0cm) from the neck point and square up 13" (33cm) (D). Curve the line D-C into the shoulder seam at B. Join D-A and mark the centre point, (E). Square out approx 2" (5.0cm) from E (F) as a guide for drawing the curve. Curve from A to D, passing through F.

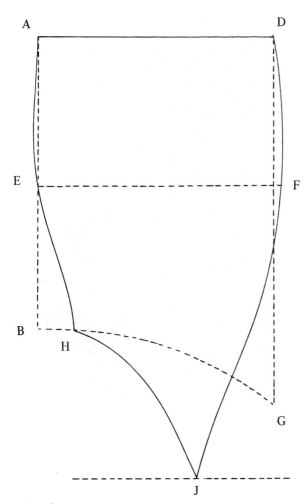

diag 8

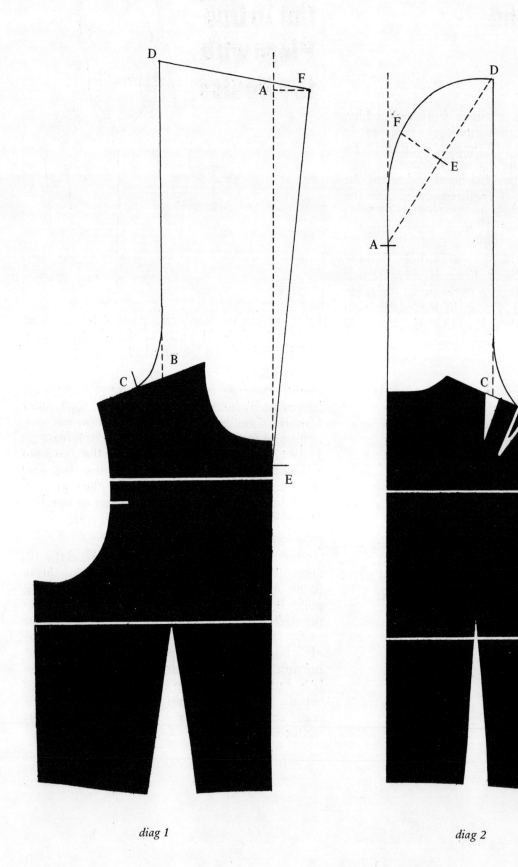

diag 1

diag 2

Collars

Upper collars
Flat collars
   Peter Pan
   Sailor
   Eton
   Jabot
Rolled collars
   Basic rolled collar
   Convertible rolled collar
Shawl collars
   Shawl collar with high stand
   Shawl collar with low stand
   (flat shawl)
   Curved shawl collar
Polo collar

Stand collar
Shirt collar
Built-up neckline
Cowl necklines
   loose-fitting cowl
   close-fitting cowl

Collars

A collar gives a garment a focal point and provides a frame for the face, and is also functional in that it is a method of finishing the neckline neatly. A garment with a collar is often more flattering than a collarless neckline. The collar style should be chosen to suit face shape, hairstyle and the remainder of the garment. A dress collar must be designed so that it will not be crushed when it is worn under a coat.

Most collars are cut separately and sewn to the neckline of the garment but shawl collars (page 83) are cut in one piece with the front bodice. The direction of the grain on a collar depends on the effect required and the fabric being used, but in general a collar is cut on the straight grain when a crisp effect is required and on the bias when a softer effect is required.

The following terms are used in making collar patterns and enable the instructions to be simplified (see diag 1):

neck edge—the edge of the collar which is stitched to the neckline of the garment

outer edge—also known as the style line as it determines the finished shape of the collar

roll line—the line along which a rolled collar folds over

stand—that part of a rolled collar which stands above the neckline, from the roll line to the neck edge

fall—the remaining part of a rolled collar, from the roll line to the outer edge.

In spite of the many variations in shape, height of stand, etc, most collar shapes belong to one of three groups:

Flat collars (page 76) turn away from the neck and lie flat on the shoulders, e.g. Peter Pan collars. A flat collar has little or no stand and may be of any width up to 6" (12.7 cm).

Rolled collars (page 81) stand above the neckline for part of their width and then fold over. A rolled collar has a very low stand at the c/f (approximately ¼" (6mm)) but a higher stand at the c/b and shoulder. The height of the stand may vary from ¾"-2" (19mm-5.0cm).

Stand collars (page 88) stand above the neckline all round and do not fold over. They are also called Mandarin collars and are usually narrow, as they would otherwise be uncomfortable to wear.

Since the length of the neck edge of the collar must be the same as the neckline of the garment, the various collar shapes are obtained by increasing or decreasing the length of the *outer* edge of the collar pattern. This changes the shape of the neck edge curve but its length always remains the same.

A flat collar has a neck edge which is very similar in shape to the neckline of the garment, a rolled collar has a less curved neck edge resulting in a shorter outer edge, a stand collar has a neck

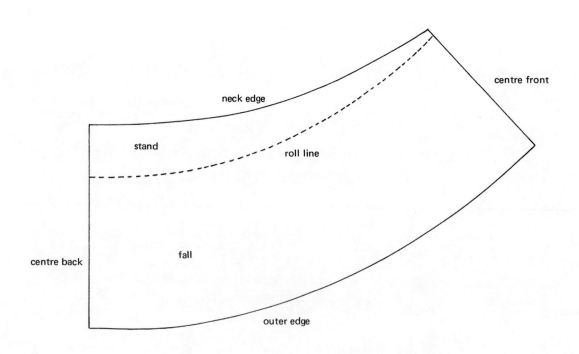

diag 1

edge which curves in the opposite direction to that of the neckline, and a jabot collar has a neck edge which is more sharply curved than the neckline. Diag 2 illustrates the comparative shapes of various collar styles.

Order of work for making a collar pattern:

1 If the collar is to be set on to a lowered neckline, draw the new neckline shape on front and back bodice blocks. Tighten the neckline, if necessary, as shown on page 45.

2 Decide on the type of collar required—flat, rolled or stand—or if working from a sketch or photograph analyse the design for type of collar, height of stand, width and shape of outer edge, etc.

3 Depending on the type chosen, either place the front and back blocks together and trace the necklines (for a flat collar) or draw the basic rectangle (for rolled and stand collars).

4 Shape the collar by increasing or decreasing the length of the outer edge as described for the chosen collar style.

5 Draw the required shape of the outer edge, remembering to measure from the roll line, if any, not the neck edge since only the part of the collar between the roll line and the outer edge will be visible.

6 Make the upper collar pattern as shown on page 74.

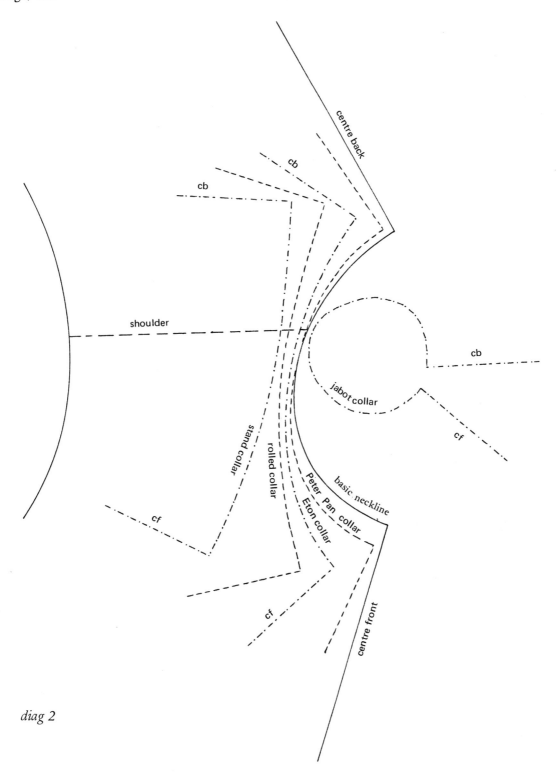

diag 2

Upper Collars

Most collars are formed of two layers of fabric, known as the upper collar and under collar, and the second layer provides a means of neatening the outer edge. (Occasionally a collar may be made from a single layer and the edge finished with binding or a decorative stitch.)

The two layers are not identical—the upper collar *must* be larger to prevent the seam around the outer edge showing when the garment is worn and, in the case of flat and rolled collars, to allow sufficient fabric for the upper collar to curve over the under collar. If the two layers are exactly the same size, the outer edge will curl up when the collar is attached, which is a very unattractive defect.

All the instructions for making the various types of collar pattern refer to the *under* collar, and the upper collar should be made as shown below. The amount needed to be added to the under collar depends on the weight of the fabric to be used (a larger amount must be added for a heavier fabric) and the style of the collar (see below).

Stand collars

A stand collar needs extra fabric allowed to hide the seam around the top edge and the seams along the c/f and c/b.

Outline the under collar (black shape in diag 1), marking c/f, c/b and shoulder line. Add $\frac{1}{8}$-$\frac{1}{4}$" (3mm-6mm) to the c/f and c/b edges (unless either is to be placed to a fold, in which case nothing is added) and $\frac{1}{8}$"-$\frac{3}{8}$" (3mm-9mm) to the outer edge. The c/f and c/b edges of the upper collar should not usually be more than $\frac{1}{8}$" (3mm) longer than those of the under collar, as it would be difficult to ease in a greater amount along such a short edge. Nothing is added to the neck edge.

Flat and rolled collars

Flat and rolled collars need extra fabric allowed on the upper collar for two reasons—to hide the seam around the outer edge and c/f edge and to enable the upper collar to curve over the under collar. They therefore need a larger amount added than stand collars.

Outline the under collar (black shape in diag 2), marking c/f, c/b, shoulder and roll line. Add $\frac{1}{8}$"-$\frac{5}{8}$" (3mm-6mm) to the c/f edge and $\frac{1}{4}$"-$\frac{3}{4}$" (6mm-19mm) to the outer edge, according to fabric. (The c/b edge is usually placed to a fold and therefore has nothing added.) Curve the outer edge upwards at the c/f so that the c/f edge of the upper collar is not more than $\frac{1}{4}$" (6mm) longer than that of the under collar. Nothing is added to the neck edge.

The placing of the straight grain on the upper collar will depend on the fabric being used and the effect required, but the under collars of coats and jackets should always be cut on the bias to ensure a soft roll and a close fit at the back of the neck. Interfacing is likewise cut on the bias and should be cut from the under collar pattern since it is attached to the under collar.

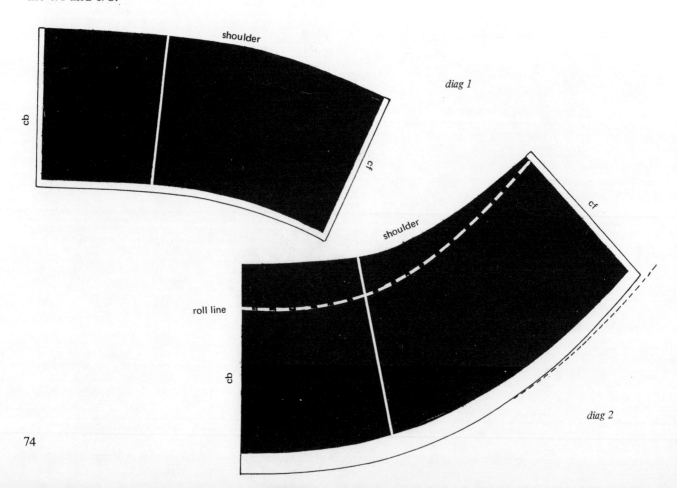

diag 1

roll line

diag 2

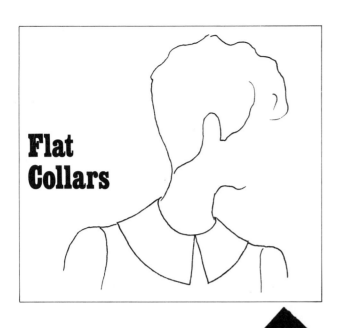

Flat Collars

Peter Pan collar

A Peter Pan collar lies flat on the shoulders and has only sufficient 'stand' to conceal the neckline seam (¼" or less). The stand in this case could more accurately be described as a 'roll' since it exists all round the collar, not just at the back. The collar may be the same width all round, or wider at the front or back as required, and the ends of the collar may be pointed or rounded. A very wide pointed Peter Pan collar is known as a Puritan collar.

Outline the front and back bodice blocks with neck points together and shoulder points overlapping ¼" (6mm). (The back shoulder point will extend beyond the front shoulder point due to the ease allowed and the dart. The dart should be ignored when making the collar pattern.) Raise the neckline ⅛" (3mm) all round—this makes the neck edge of the collar slightly shorter than the neckline of the garment and stretching the collar on to the neckline helps to produce a slight roll. The roll hides the neckline seam and also prevents the outer edge of the collar buckling. Measure the width of the collar as required from the neckline and shape the ends of the collar. The straight grain line may be parallel to the c/b, c/f or shoulder, according to the effect required.

75

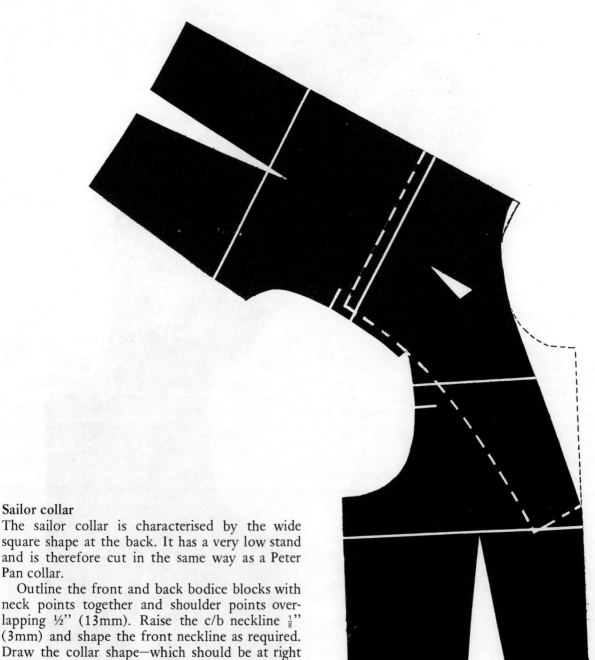

Sailor collar

The sailor collar is characterised by the wide square shape at the back. It has a very low stand and is therefore cut in the same way as a Peter Pan collar.

Outline the front and back bodice blocks with neck points together and shoulder points overlapping ½" (13mm). Raise the c/b neckline ⅛" (3mm) and shape the front neckline as required. Draw the collar shape—which should be at right angles to the c/b and pass through or close to the shoulder point. The shape of the front of the collar may be varied as required.

76

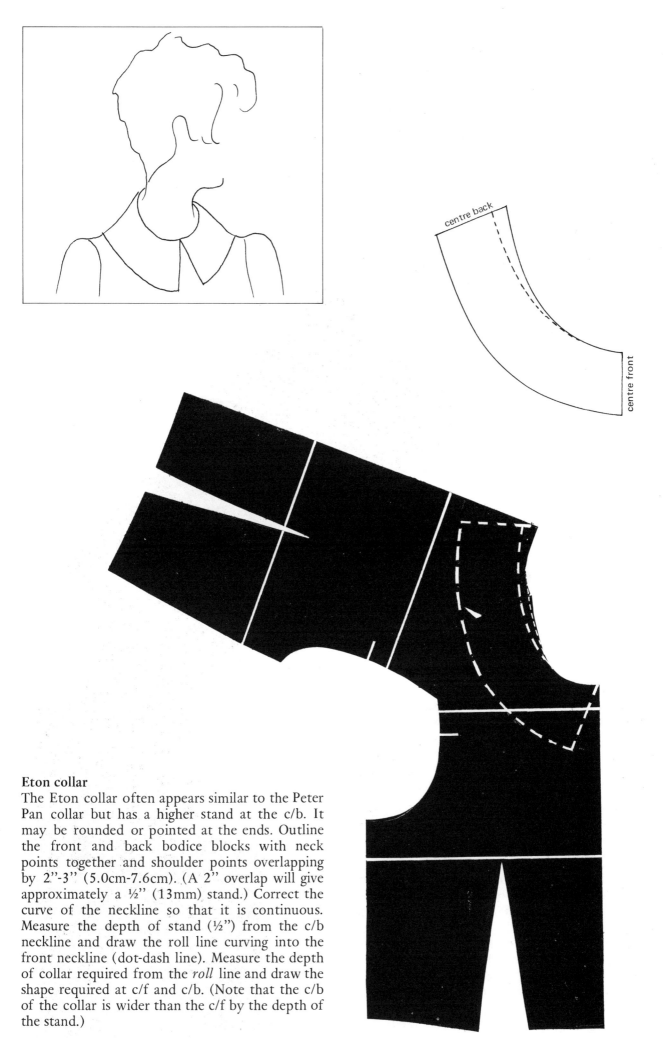

Eton collar

The Eton collar often appears similar to the Peter Pan collar but has a higher stand at the c/b. It may be rounded or pointed at the ends. Outline the front and back bodice blocks with neck points together and shoulder points overlapping by 2"-3" (5.0cm-7.6cm). (A 2" overlap will give approximately a ½" (13mm) stand.) Correct the curve of the neckline so that it is continuous. Measure the depth of stand (½") from the c/b neckline and draw the roll line curving into the front neckline (dot-dash line). Measure the depth of collar required from the *roll* line and draw the shape required at c/f and c/b. (Note that the c/b of the collar is wider than the c/f by the depth of the stand.)

centre back

centre front

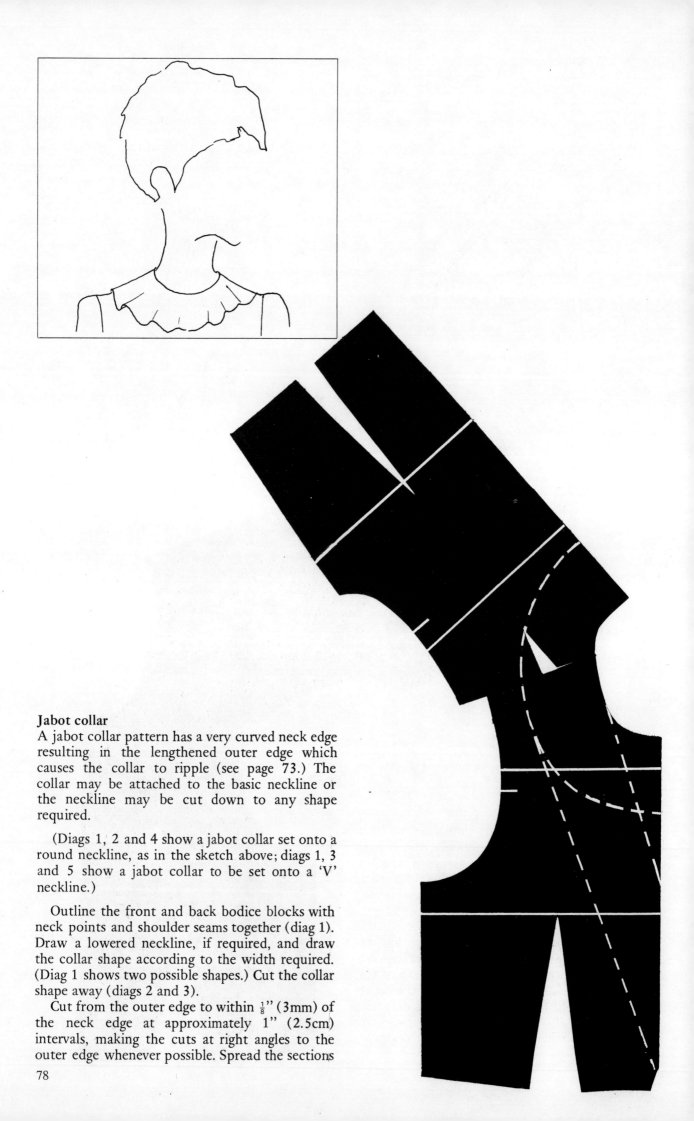

Jabot collar

A jabot collar pattern has a very curved neck edge resulting in the lengthened outer edge which causes the collar to ripple (see page 73.) The collar may be attached to the basic neckline or the neckline may be cut down to any shape required.

(Diags 1, 2 and 4 show a jabot collar set onto a round neckline, as in the sketch above; diags 1, 3 and 5 show a jabot collar to be set onto a 'V' neckline.)

Outline the front and back bodice blocks with neck points and shoulder seams together (diag 1). Draw a lowered neckline, if required, and draw the collar shape according to the width required. (Diag 1 shows two possible shapes.) Cut the collar shape away (diags 2 and 3).

Cut from the outer edge to within $\frac{1}{8}$" (3mm) of the neck edge at approximately 1" (2.5cm) intervals, making the cuts at right angles to the outer edge whenever possible. Spread the sections apart until the pattern forms a circle (diags 4 and 5) leaving at least ½" (13mm) between c/f and c/b edges for a seam allowance. Correct the curves.

(Collars made by this method will have seams as c/b and c/f—if shoulder seams are preferred, the collar shapes, (diag 2 and 3), should be cut along the shoulder seams before cutting into the neck edge, and each part spread into a quarter circle, ensuring that the amounts added at each cut are approximately equal. The c/b and c/f may then be placed to a fold.)

diag 3

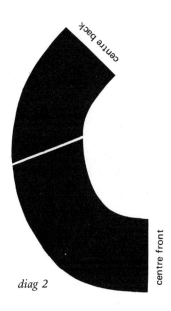

diag 2

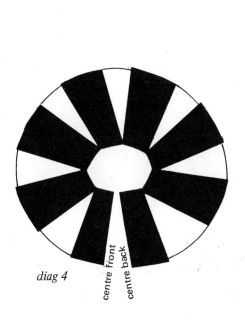

diag 4

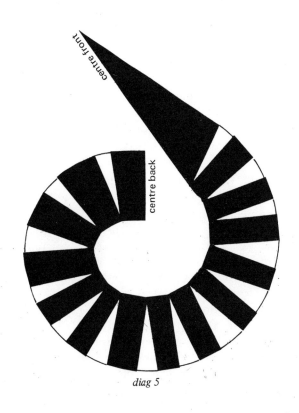

diag 5

Rolled Collar

Diag 3
Draw the basic rectangle and draw two lines between the shoulder and the c/f (G-H and J-K). Cut from F, H and K almost to the neck edge and spread the sections apart ½" (13mm) at F, ¾" (19mm) at H and 1" (2.5cm) at K. This will give a stand of approximately 1" (2.5cm). Correct the curve of the neck edge. Draw the roll line as shown, the c/f edge (D-L) at right angles to the roll line and the outer edge as required.

Diags 2 and 3 are merely intended as examples of the method of making a rolled collar and the amounts by which the outer edge is increased may be varied according to the height of stand required. Note that a slightly smaller amount is added at the shoulder (E-F) than at the other positions. The outer edge may be shaped in any way that is required—wider at c/b, wider at c/f, extending to a point at the c/f, etc.

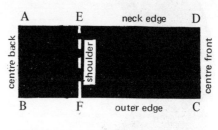

diag 1

Basic rolled collar

Rolled collars are those which stand up from the neckline at the c/b and shoulder and either continue to a very low stand at the c/f or fold back to form a 'V' shaped neckline with a lapel. A rolled collar may be designed so that it can be worn either way (page 81). The height of the stand may vary from ¾" (19mm) to 2" (5.0cm).

There are two methods of cutting rolled collars—by tracing the necklines of the blocks and tightening the outer edge, as for an Eton collar (page 77), or by adapting from the basic rectangle. The latter method is used here.

Draw the basic rectangle, which should be the length of the neckline m/ment of the blocks by the depth of fall required at the c/f (diag 1). Mark the shoulder line, c/f and c/b. This rectangle may be used as a collar pattern without further adaptation (see page 81) but the stand will be very high—equal to approximately half of the c/b width. To make the stand lower, the outer edge must be lengthened by cutting and spreading.

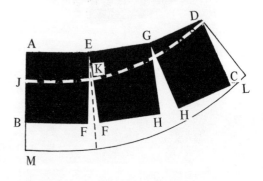

diag 2

Diag 2
Draw the basic rectangle and draw a line mid-way between the shoulder and the c/f at right angles to the neck edge (G-H). Cut from G and F almost to the neck edge and spread the sections apart ½" (13mm) at F and ¾" (19mm) at H. This will give a stand of approximately 1¼" (3.1cm). Correct the curve of the neck edge. Measure 1¼" (3.1cm) down from A (J) and approximately 1" (2.5cm) from E (K) and curve to ¼" (6mm) below D for the roll line. Draw the new c/f line (D-L) at right angles to the roll line or as required. (Remember that only the part of the collar between the roll line and the outer edge is visible when the collar is worn.)

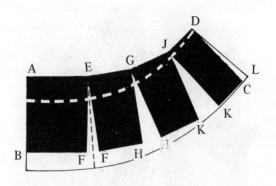

diag 3

Convertible rolled collar

This type of collar may either be worn open, forming a 'V' neckline with a notched collar, as shown in the first sketch, or closed as shown in the second sketch. Note that the collar forms a 'V' shape at the c/f when worn closed, as opposed to the examples on the previous pages which curve to the shape of the neck.

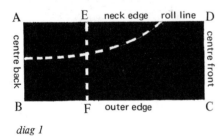

diag 1

The basic rectangle may be used to make this collar (diag 1) and is perfectly satisfactory when the collar is worn open but has a very high stand (equal to approximately half the c/b width) and tends to stand away from the neck, particularly at the back, when worn closed. It is also considerably narrower at the c/b than at the c/f when worn closed.

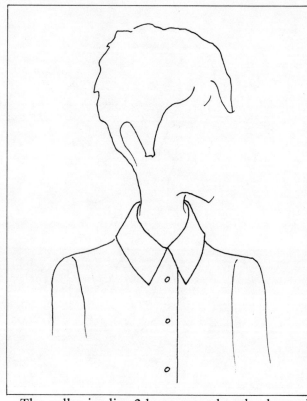

The collar in diag 2 has a curved neck edge and a straight roll line, which gives a better fit. Draw a

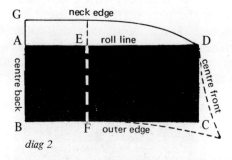

diag 2

rectangle (A-B-C-D) measuring the neckline m/ment of the bodice blocks less ¼" (6mm), by the depth of fall required at the c/b. Extend the c/b 1" (2.5cm) upwards (or as required) (G) for the height of the stand and square across. Curve the neck edge down to D from just beyond the shoulder line.

The basic pattern gives a collar which is even in width all round but the outer edge and c/f edge may be extended to form any shape of collar required, as shown by the broken lines.

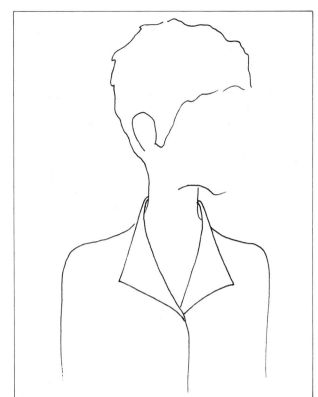

Shawl collars

A shawl collar differs from all other types in that the under collar is cut in one piece with the front bodice and the upper collar is cut in one piece with the front facing. This type of collar may also be called a rever collar or a roll collar.

A shawl collar may lie flat on the shoulders, like a Peter Pan collar, or it may have a stand, which can vary from ¼" (6mm) to 2" (5.0cm). As with all collars, the height of the stand is controlled by the length of the outer edge: the longer the outer edge, the lower the stand. The shawl collar is most often used in the classic 'dressing gown' shape as shown in the first sketch, although many variations are possible, as shown.

Shawl collar with a high stand

Outline the front bodice block allowing a margin of approximately 6" (15.2cm) above it. Add the required width of overlap to the c/f (see page . . .) and draw the roll line, A-B, passing ½" (13mm) from the neck point and extending approximately 4" (10.2cm) above it.

Place the back bodice *face downwards* with neck points together and c/b neck point (C) overlapping the roll line by approximately ½" (13mm). Outline the back neckline and part of the c/b. Measure the depth of collar required from C along the c/b, allowing for a 1"-1½" (2.5cm-3.8cm) stand. Curve the outer edge of the collar smoothly into the front edge just above A. (The outer edge of the collar must join to the c/b with a right angle to ensure that the curve of the entire collar is continuous.) Folding the collar back along the roll line will give an impression of the finished shape.

Although the collar is drafted in one piece with the front bodice, a better fit is usually obtained by joining the neck point (D) to point A and cutting along that line to separate the bodice and collar (See diag 2). This avoids having to clip the fabric at the neck point when making up and thus causing a weak point which may tear. The upper collar and facing are cut in one piece, as shown in diag 3; this gives less strain on the neck point of the facing and achieves the desired all-in-one effect.

Facing

Draw the facing line on the bodice (dot-dash line in diag 1), making the facing approx 2" (5.0cm) wide at the shoulder and 3" (7.6cm) at the hem. Trace the front edge, collar and facing line to make the facing pattern as shown in diag 3. As the facing also forms the upper collar, the outer edge must be increased as described on page 75. Curve the new outer edge into the front edge at point H.

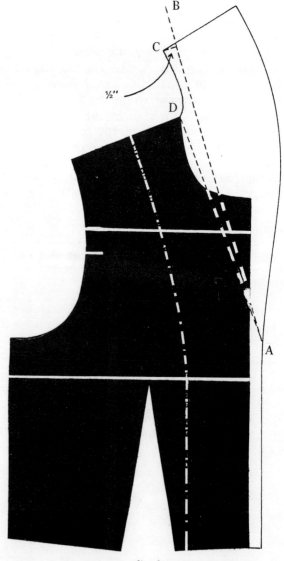

diag 1

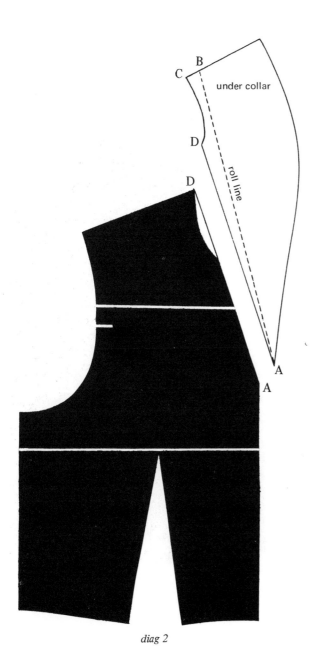

diag 2

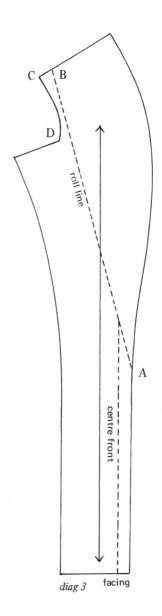

diag 3

Shawl collar with a low stand

This collar has a stand of ¾"-1" (19mm-2.5cm) which is achieved by overlapping the back bodice and the roll line by a larger amount than in the previous example. Proceed as for the shawl collar with a high stand but place the back bodice to overlap the roll line by approx 1½" (3.8cm).

Flat shawl collar

This collar resembles a Peter Pan collar in that it lies flat on the shoulders with only sufficient stand to hide the seam at the back of the neck. Outline the front bodice block, add the overlap to the front edge and draw the roll line as for the two previous adaptations. Place the back bodice block face downwards with neck points together and the c/b almost parallel to the c/f (there should be approximately a ½" (13mm) gap between the guide line and the c/b at D). Measure the depth of collar required from C, allowing ¼" (6mm) for the stand. Curve from D into the front edge according to the collar shape required.

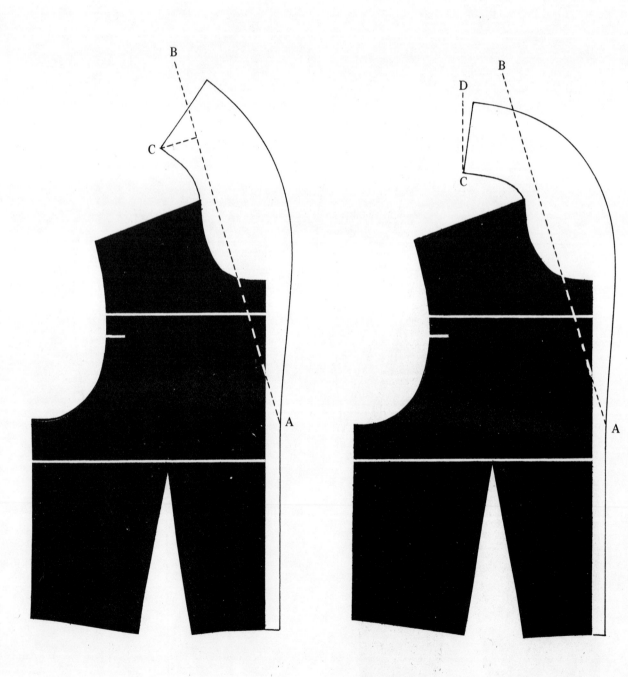

Curved shawl collar

The shawl collar methods described so far give a collar with a straight roll line, as shown in the left hand sketch. To make the roll line curved—draw a line from the neck point parallel to the roll line (D-E, diag 1) and mark the centre point (F). Measure ¼"-½" (6mm-13mm) each side of F (according to the amount of curve required) (G and H). Curve D-G-E and D-H-E and cut along the curved lines to separate the front bodice from the collar, as shown in diag 2.

Trace the bodice section as shown on page 85 to make the front facing pattern and trace the collar section (increasing the size as described on page 75) for the upper collar pattern.

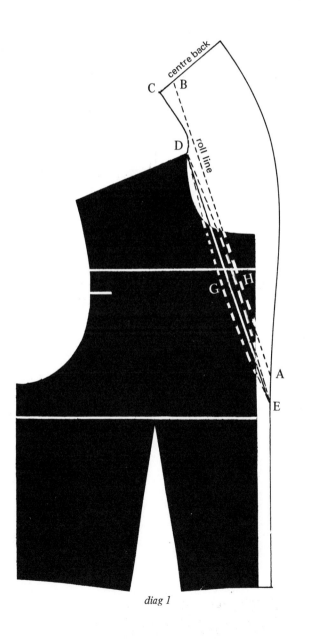

diag 1

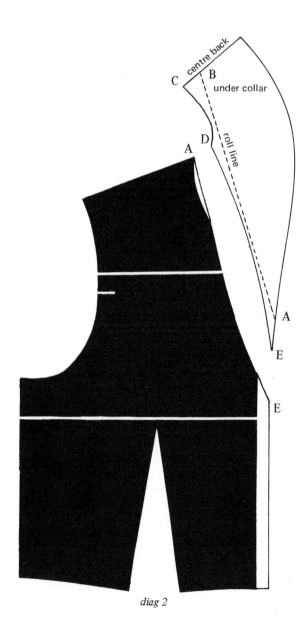

diag 2

Polo Collar

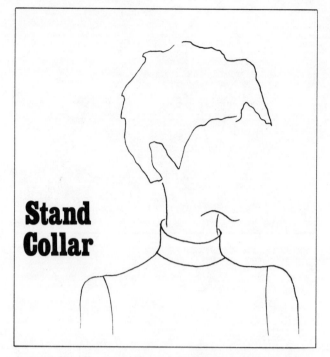

Stand Collar

The polo collar is strictly a rolled collar since it stands up from the neckline and folds over, but it is cut simply from a rectangle of fabric. It should be cut on the bias whenever possible to ensure that it folds softly and smoothly. The width of the pattern must be four times the width of the finished collar, which is usually approx 2" (5.0cm). Because the collar is to be cut on the bias the pattern must be for the *entire* collar—not one-half, as on most collar patterns.

Measure the necklines of front and back blocks and double the m/ment.

Decide on the finished width required and multiply by four. Draw a rectangle from these m/ments, marking c/f, shoulder seams and the fold lines of the collar. Draw the straight grain line at 45° to the c/b.

A stand collar stands up from the neckline but, unlike the polo collar, does not fold over. The collar may be continuous across the c/f or it may have a slit at the c/f. The top edge *must* be shorter than the neck edge, usually by 1"-1½" (2.5cm-3.8cm), to enable the collar to fit closely to the side of the neck. A stand collar made from a straight strip of fabric will fit very badly at the c/b and the side front.

Measure the necklines of front and back blocks and draw a rectangle A-B-C-D the length of the neckline m/ment by the width of collar required (diag 1). Mark the shoulder line (E-F) and cut out the rectangle.

Mark point G approx 1½" (3.8cm) from D and point H 1½" (3.8cm) from G. Square down to the lower edge. Fold three darts in the top edge, at E, H and G, each approximately ¼" (6mm) wide, and a smaller dart between E and A until the top edge measures the required amount. Trace the pattern on to a new sheet of paper and correct the curves. (Diag 2).

There are four possible positions for the straight grain line—parallel to the c/f or c/b or at right angles to the c/f or c/b—according to the fabric and style of the dress.

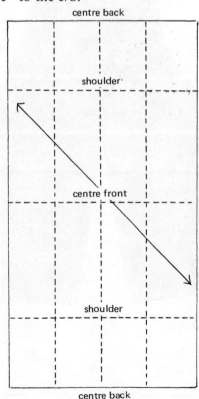

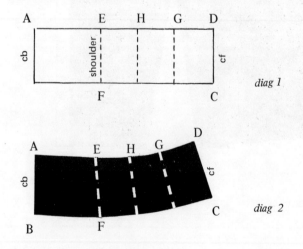

diag 1

diag 2

Shirt Collar

An authentic shirt collar is cut in two parts—with the stand separate from the fall—and therefore has a seam along the top edge. This enables the collar to fit very closely, especially around the top edge. The method shown on page 82, diag 2, may be used to make a simpler one-piece shirt collar but it will not fit as well as the two-piece collar.

Stand (also called collar band)
The stand may be the same height all round, or wider at the c/b: for example, 1½" (3.8cm) at the c/b and 1" (2.5cm) at the c/f.

The pattern is made in the same way as the stand collar on page 88, but with an extension added to the c/f for the stand to overlap and button (diag 1). The amount added should be the same as added to the c/f of the bodice for overlap (see page 52). Curve the top edge of the extension G-H as shown in diag 1.

Collar
Measure the top edge of the stand, to the c/f only (A-G). (The top edge of the collar must measure the same as the top edge of the stand.) The collar must be at least ¼" (6mm) wider than the stand all round so that the neckline seam is covered, but should not be more than ½" (13mm) wider. Draw a rectangle J-K-L-M, with J-M equal to A-G (top edge of the stand) and J-K ¼" (6mm) greater than A-B (diag 2).

Mark the shoulder line (N-P). Move point L out ¼" (6mm) (Q) and curve the front edge of the collar from M through Q, continuing to the required length. Draw the shape of the front collar as required—pointed, rounded, etc. Mark point R on the top edge 1" (2.5cm) from M and point S 1½" (3.8cm) from R. Square down to the lower edge (T and U). Cut out the pattern and cut from points P, T and U to within $\frac{1}{8}$" (3mm) of N, S and R. Spread the sections apart, adding ½" (13mm) at the line R-U and ¼" (6mm) at each of the other two lines, (diag 3). Trace the collar on to a new sheet of paper.

Diags 1 and 3 show the finished stand and collar patterns.

shoulder

A E G
B F C H

diag 1

J N S R M
K P T L Q
U

diag 2

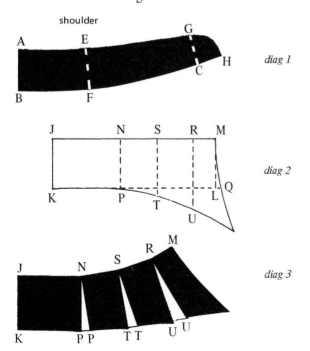

M
R
S
J N
K P P T T U U

diag 3

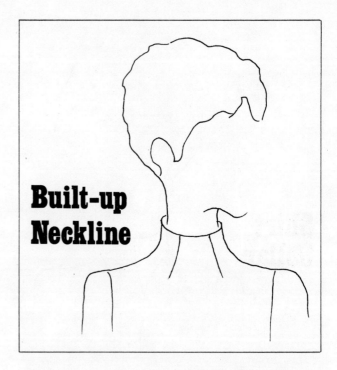

Built-up Neckline

A built-up neckline may be continuous across the front, or it may have a slit at the front. This adaptation gives a neckline which stands away slightly from the neck but the darts may be tightened at the top edge if a closer fit is required. Outline the front bodice block and mark point A approximately 2" (5.0cm) from the c/f neck point, (diag 1). Join A to the bust point and cut along that line. Fold out part of the waist dart until there is a 1" (25mm) wide dart at A (diag 2). Raise the c/f neck point 2" (5.0cm) (or as required but not less than 1½" (3.8cm) if the style is to be effective) and mark point B. Square up 1½" (3.8cm) from the neck point and mark point C. From C, square out 1" (25mm) towards the c/f (D). Curve from D into the shoulder seam approx 2" (5.0cm) from the original neck point and curve from D to B as shown. Mark the centre point of the neckline dart. Join to the bust point and continue the line upwards to the top edge of the pattern (broken line). The finished neckline dart should extend almost to the top edge and should be the same length below A as above.

Outline the back bodice block and mark point E approximately 1½" (3.8cm) from the c/b neck point (diag 3). Join to the point of the waist dart and cut along the line. Fold out part of the waist dart until the neckline dart is ¾" (19mm) wide (diag 4). Raise the c/b neck point 2" (5.0cm) (F) and square out a guide line. Square up 1½" (3.8cm) from the neck point (G) and square out 1¼" (3.1cm) towards the c/b (H). Curve from H into the shoulder seam and to F, as shown. Mark the centre point of the dart and join to the point of the waist dart. Continue the line to the top edge of the pattern and draw the neckline dart as on the front pattern.

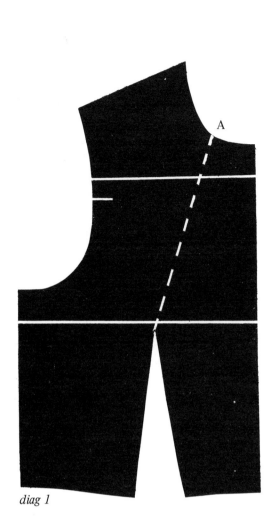

diag 1

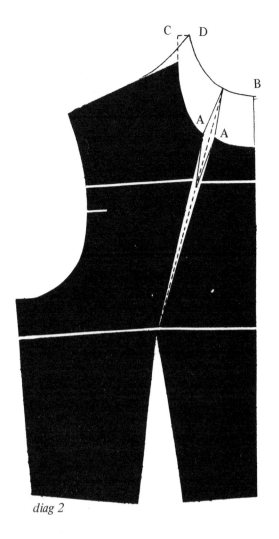

diag 2

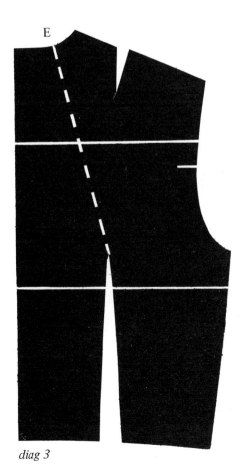

diag 3

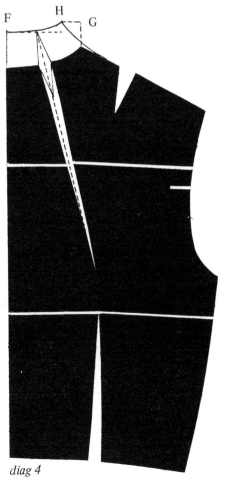

diag 4

91

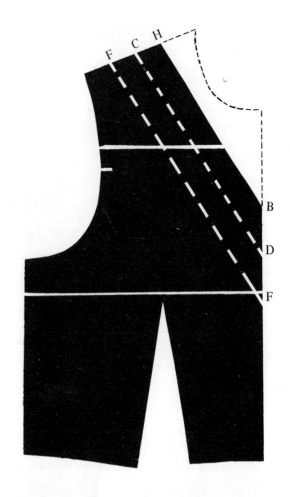

Cowl necklines are formed by soft, curving folds of fabric at the front or back of the bodice. The depth of the neckline may be varied by raising or lowering the neckline before planning the cowl. The bodice should always be cut on the bias for the most attractive effect, and soft light-weight fabrics must be used.

Loose-fitting cowl

Outline the front bodice block and draw a lowered neckline as required (line A-B). Draw two lines parallel to the new neckline and 1" (2.5cm) apart (C-D and E-F). Cut along the lines from the c/f to within $\frac{1}{8}$" (3mm) of C and E.

Draw two lines at right angles on a new sheet of paper to represent the c/f and neckline of the pattern. Place the line A-B to the top line but with the point C to the c/f line (this allows a small amount of additional ease across the neckline). Spread the sections apart until the c/f waist point (G) is on the c/f line (diag 2). Cut off the protruding point F.

The c/f must be placed on the bias.

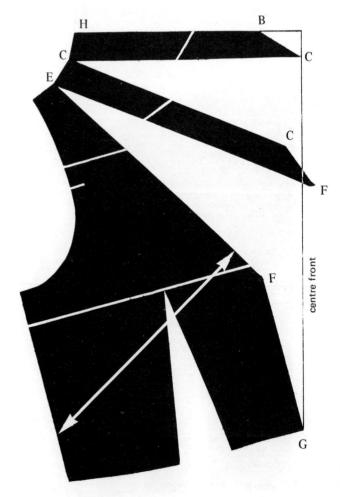

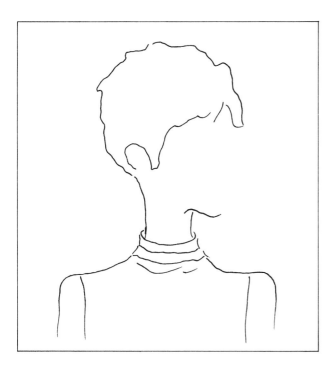

Close-fitting cowl

The close-fitting cowl stands up around the neck and the folds are therefore smaller and tighter than in the deeper cowls.

Outline the front bodice block and adapt it to a built-up neckline as shown on page   . Join the neck point (A) to the c/f neck point (B) with a straight line. Mark point C 1'' (2.5cm) below B and point D 2'' (5.0cm) below on the c/f. Mark points E and F on the shoulder seam, 1'' (2.5cm) apart. Join C-E and D-F with curved lines, (diag 1).

Cut along the lines D-F and C-E from the c/f to within $\frac{1}{8}$'' (3mm) of the shoulder. Draw two lines at right angles on a new sheet of paper to represent the c/f and neckline of the pattern. Place C at the angle of the lines and spread the sections apart until the c/f waist point (G) is on the c/f line, (diag 2). Cut off the protruding point D and correct the curve of the shoulder seam.

The c/f must be placed on the bias.

Outline the back bodice block and adapt it to a built-up neckline. The back may then be adapted to a cowl as above or left as it is, as required.

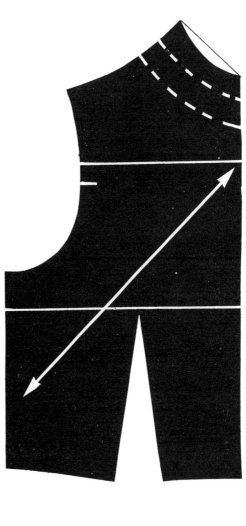

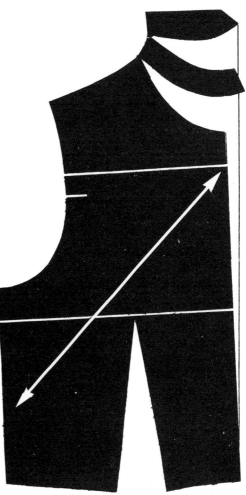

Sleeves

Semi-fitting sleeve
Tight fitting sleeve
Elbow darts
Short sleeve
Three-quarter length sleeve
Bishop sleeves—methods 1, 2, 3 and 4
Bell sleeve
Peasant sleeve
Wrist opening
Raised sleeveheads:
    puffed sleeves—methods 1, 2 and 3
    darted sleevehead
    gathered sleevehead—methods 1 and 2
    Leg o'mutton sleeve
    sleeve with inset band
    sleeve with joined band
    sleeve with curved band
Long frilled sleeve
Shallow sleevehead
Two-piece sleeve
Raglan sleeves:
    high raglan
    low raglan
    deep raglan
Drop shoulders:
    high drop shoulder
    low drop shoulder
Square armhole—methods 1 and 2
Deep armhole
Kimono sleeves:
    kimono block
Gussets:
    diamond shaped gusset
    strip gusset
    shortened strip gusset
    gusset incorporated in a yoke—methods 1 and 2
    gusset incorporated in a panel seam
Dolman or bat-wing sleeve
Magyar or cap sleeve

Sleeves

Sleeves are classified and take their names from the way in which they join on to the a/h: set-in sleeves, raglan, drop-shoulder, etc; or by their width at the wrist: tight-fitting, bishop etc. A third group is those which are cut in one piece with the bodice, such as kimono and dolman.

The basic set-in sleeve is the most commonly used because it is the most comfortable to wear and the best fit in most arm positions. This is because the seam joining the sleeve to the bodice passes around the shoulder and under the arm. This enables extra length to be incorporated under the arm to allow it to be raised easily and without the dress being lifted at the hem.

A set-in sleeve may be eased into the a/h, giving a smooth line over the shoulder, or the s/h may be made to stand up by gathering, pleating or darting it into the a/h according to the shape required at the shoulder. If a plain (eased) s/h is required, the m/ment around the s/h must always be *at least* 1" (2.5cm) greater than the m/ment around the a/h, and the aim should be to ease in as much fabric as possible without causing the s/h to pucker. The amount will vary according to the fabric—a loosely woven woollen might allow as much as 3" (7.6cm) to be eased in, whereas in a firm cotton 1" (2.5cm) might be the maximum which could be successfully eased in without the s/h puckering. The s/h should only be eased over the shoulder between the front and back balance marks, and the lower part of the sleeve, under the arm, should be set in without ease. A sleeve which had no ease over the shoulder would look very unattractive as it would pull and crease over the shoulder bone.

The sleeve block shown here is completely straight at the sides, which makes adaptation very much easier, but it should rarely be used as a pattern without any adaptation as it would appear rather shapeless. The sleeve block should not be made into a close-fitting sleeve by simply taking in the side seams as a poor shape would result and there would be insufficient room for the elbow to bend. A close-fitting sleeve should always have at least one elbow dart (see pages 98 and 99), or alternatively the sleeve may be cut in two sections with a seam at the back of the arm (see page 121). The latter gives a very attractive shape and fit, following the curve of the arm, and is most frequently used for coats and jackets.

The basic raglan sleeve is formed by detaching part of the bodice pattern and joining it to the sleeve pattern; and the high drop-shoulder style uses the same principle in reverse—part of the sleeve pattern is cut away and joined to the bodice pattern. (See pages 124 to 128). Since in both these cases the u/arm curves of both bodice and sleeve remain unaltered, the high raglan and high drop-shoulder styles fit as well as a set-in sleeve. The deep raglan is cut with a lower a/h and the low raglan and low drop-shoulder are cut from the kimono block and therefore fit more loosely.

Although the term 'kimono' sleeve strictly refers to the type of sleeve found on Japanese kimonos—very loose, wide at the hem and cut low under the arm—the name is often used to describe any sleeve which is cut in one piece with the bodice. Kimono sleeves are explained in more detail on page 136.

In the sleeve adaptations which follow, the straight grain line is always parallel to the centre line, unless otherwise stated.

Semifitting Sleeve

Suitable for a dress or jacket when a shaped, but not closely fitting, sleeve is required.
Outline the sleeve block.

To shape the sleeve on the elbow line—measure in approximately ¾" (19mm) from the front side seam (A) and join to the u/arm and wrist with a smoothly curved line. Measure in approximately ½" (13mm) from the back side seam (B) and join to the u/arm with a straight line.

Wrist shaping
Cut along the elbow line as far as the back arm line and fold a dart along the lower part of the back arm line, so that a dart opens on the elbow line. The dart should not be wider than 1" (2.5cm). Measure in up to 1½" (3.8cm) (according to the wrist m/ment required) along the wrist line from the back side seam (C) and join to B with a straight line.

The amounts cut away at points A, B and C may be varied according to the shape required, but the wrist line should not measure less than 9" (22.9cm) and the elbow line not less than 12½" (32cm) or the sleeve will be uncomfortable to wear (unless it is made in knitted fabric, in which case the m/ments could be reduced by 1"-2" (2.5cm-5.0cm)). The black shape in the diagram shows the finished pattern, and the broken lines show the original block.

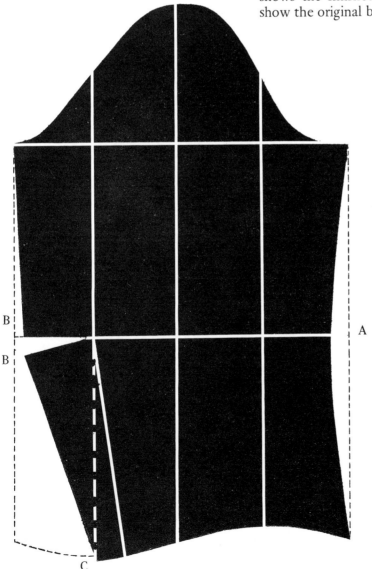

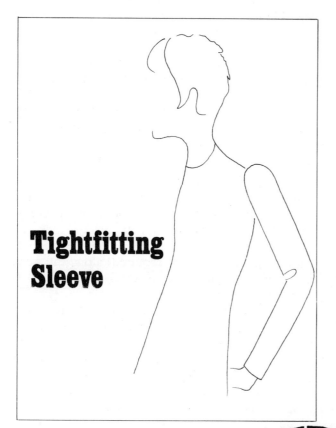

Tightfitting Sleeve

This sleeve is suitable for dresses or blouses only as it would need a wrist opening in the side seam or along the back arm line.

Outline the sleeve block.

Elbow shaping

Measure in approximately ¾" (19mm) from the front side seam along the elbow line (A) and curve smoothly to the u/arm and wrist.

Wrist shaping

Measure in 1½" (3.8cm) along the wrist line from the back side seam (B) and join to the u/arm with a straight line.

Cut along the elbow line as far as the front arm line and fold a dart along each of the three construction lines—front arm line, centre line and back arm line. A dart will then open on the elbow line. The widths of the three darts may be varied to obtain the required m/ment of the wrist line, but this should not be less than wrist m/ment plus 1" (2.5cm). It is preferable to fold slightly wider darts on the back arm and centre lines than on the front arm line. The dart which opens on the elbow line is too wide to be sewn as one dart and must be made into two or three smaller darts as shown on the following page.

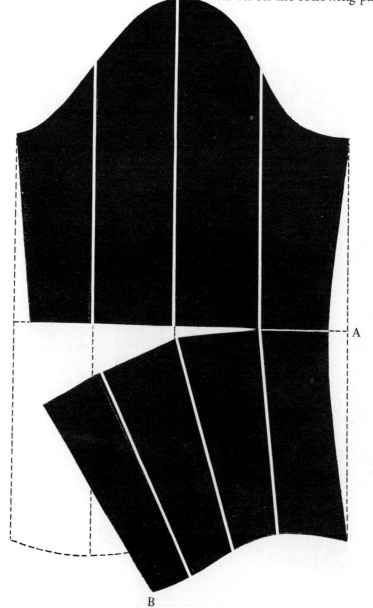

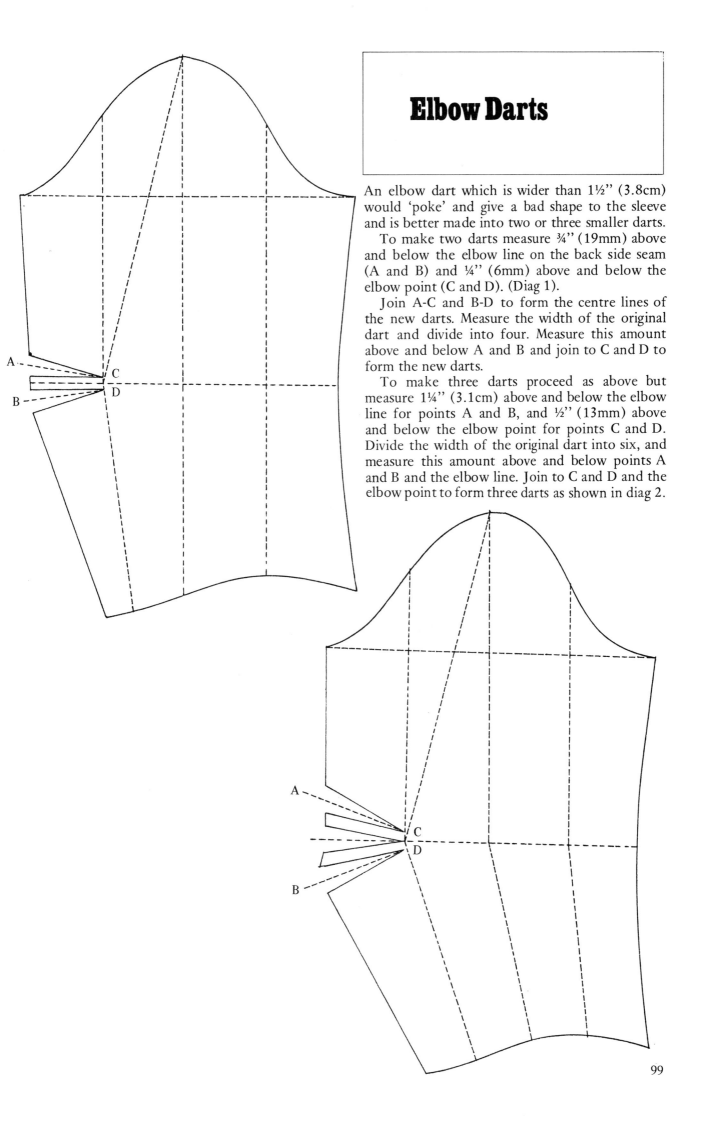

Elbow Darts

An elbow dart which is wider than 1½" (3.8cm) would 'poke' and give a bad shape to the sleeve and is better made into two or three smaller darts.

To make two darts measure ¾" (19mm) above and below the elbow line on the back side seam (A and B) and ¼" (6mm) above and below the elbow point (C and D). (Diag 1).

Join A-C and B-D to form the centre lines of the new darts. Measure the width of the original dart and divide into four. Measure this amount above and below A and B and join to C and D to form the new darts.

To make three darts proceed as above but measure 1¼" (3.1cm) above and below the elbow line for points A and B, and ½" (13mm) above and below the elbow point for points C and D. Divide the width of the original dart into six, and measure this amount above and below points A and B and the elbow line. Join to C and D and the elbow point to form three darts as shown in diag 2.

Short Sleeve

Outline the sleeve block and cut across at the required length, parallel to the u/arm line. Although the pattern thus obtained could be used for a short sleeve without further adaptation, it is not advisable as it would be loose at the lower edge.

Determine the required width of the lower edge—by measuring around the arm at the required sleeve length and adding 2'' (5.0cm) for ease. Crease the pattern on the front and back arm lines and fold a dart along each line until the lower edge measures the required amount. The two darts should be equal in width. Correct the line of the s/head and the lower edge, which will now be curved.

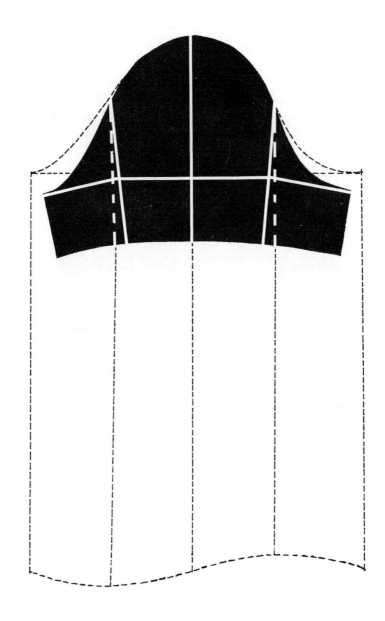

Three Quarter Length Sleeve

Outline the sleeve block and cut across at the required length, parallel to the wrist line.

(Remember to measure the length with the arm bent or the sleeve will ride up and be too short when the arm is bent.)

Follow the instructions for a semi-fitting sleeve on page 96, making the width at the lower edge as required but not less than 11" (27.9cm).

Bishop Sleeve

A bishop sleeve is one which is eased, gathered or pleated into a cuff at the wrist. The width of the sleeve at the wrist may vary from only slightly more than the size of the cuff, to 30"-40" (78cm-102cm) or more.

A bishop sleeve is always longer than the m/ment of the arm to allow it to blouse over at the wrist which, apart from looking more attractive, allows the arm to be stretched or raised without the cuff being pulled back along the arm. More length is added to the back of the sleeve (on the back arm line) than to the front, and also more fullness is added at the back as that is where it is most effective. The amount of length added depends on the weight of the fabric to be used but an average amount would be 2"-3" (5.0cm-7.6cm) on the back arm line and half that amount on the front arm line and the side seams. The amount of fullness also varies according to fabric: a very fine material such as chiffon can incorporate much more fullness than a woollen fabric.

Four methods of making a bishop sleeve pattern are shown on the following pages, each resulting in a subtle difference in shape. The first method has fullness added to the side seams; in all the other methods the pattern is cut and the sections spread apart to achieve fullness. The first method enables only a small amount of fullness to be added, the reason being that cutting and spreading causes the fullness to fall in the positions that the cuts are made, i.e. evenly around the sleeve, whereas an excessive amount added to the side seams would cause all the fullness to bunch around the seam and give an unattractive shape to the sleeve.

As with any adaptation involving the addition of fullness, it is impossible to describe the effect that the addition of any given amount will produce as it depends so much on the weight of the fabric. This can only be found by experimenting with varying sleeve widths in different fabrics.

Any of the methods for obtaining a bishop sleeve may be combined with any of the methods for raising the s/h (shown on page 107) if fullness is desired at the top of the sleeve in addition to the wrist. The bishop sleeve adaptation should be completed, and re-drawn on a new sheet of paper, before the raised s/h adaptation is attempted.

Bishop sleeve—1

This is the simplest method but it enables only a small amount of fullness to be added.

Outline the sleeve block. Decide on the depth of cuff to be incorporated and draw a curve across the pattern at that level parallel to the hem line (line A-B on diagram). Add approximately 2" (5.0cm) extra length to the back arm line and approximately 1" (2.5cm) to the front arm line and side seams, remembering to add on to the dotted line, not the original hem line. Curve the new hem line and cut along it (line C-D).

Measure out 2"-3" (5.0cm-7.6cm) from C (point E) and the same amount from D (point F). Join the u/arm points to E and F with straight lines. Measure the length of the side seams—from the u/arm points to C and D—then measure the same amounts from the u/arm points towards E and F and mark the new side seam length—points G and H. Draw the new hemline passing through G and H as shown and check that the curve of the hem line is continuous across the seam by folding the sides of the pattern to meet after cutting it out. The side seams may be slightly curved if preferred—fold the pattern in half lengthways and cut through double paper to ensure that the curves are identical.

No more than 3" (7.6cm) should be added to each seam by this method or the sleeve will not hang attractively. If greater fullness is required the sleeve must be cut and spread as shown on pages 102 to 105.

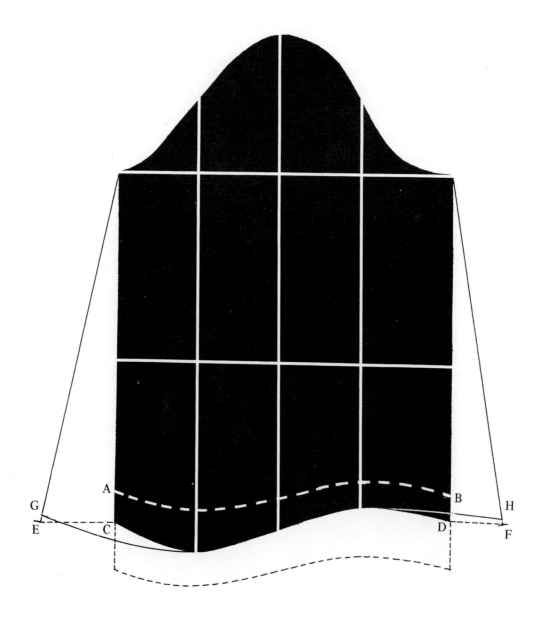

Bishop sleeve—2

This method enables the greatest amount of fullness to be added.

Outline the sleeve block and draw the new hem line, i.e. subtract the width of the cuff but add extra length for the sleeve to blouse over—3"-4" (7.6cm-10.2cm) on the back arm line and half that amount on the front arm line and the side seams. (More length may be added when using this method than when using method 1 since greater width is also being added.) Cut along the new hem line.

Cut from the hem line along the back arm line, centre line and front arm line to within $\frac{1}{8}$" (3mm) of the s/head so that the sections are just held together. Spread the sections apart until the hem line measures the required amount, remembering to add most at the back arm line (diag 1).

Correct the curve of the hem line, and the s/head.

Draw the straight grain line parallel to the new centre line, which is mid-way between the centre edges.

In theory, the sections may be spread apart until the sleeve forms a complete circle (diag 2) which will give a hem width of approx 130" (330cm). (The block has been cut into eight sections (diag 3) instead of the usual four to help with the drawing of the hem curve.)

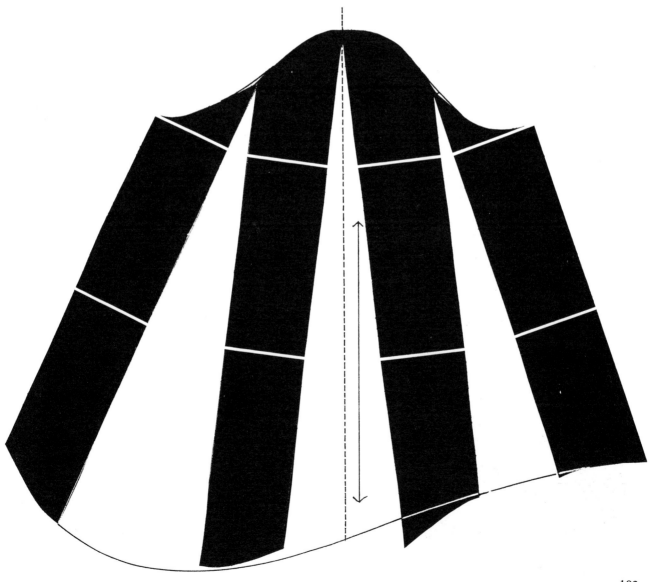

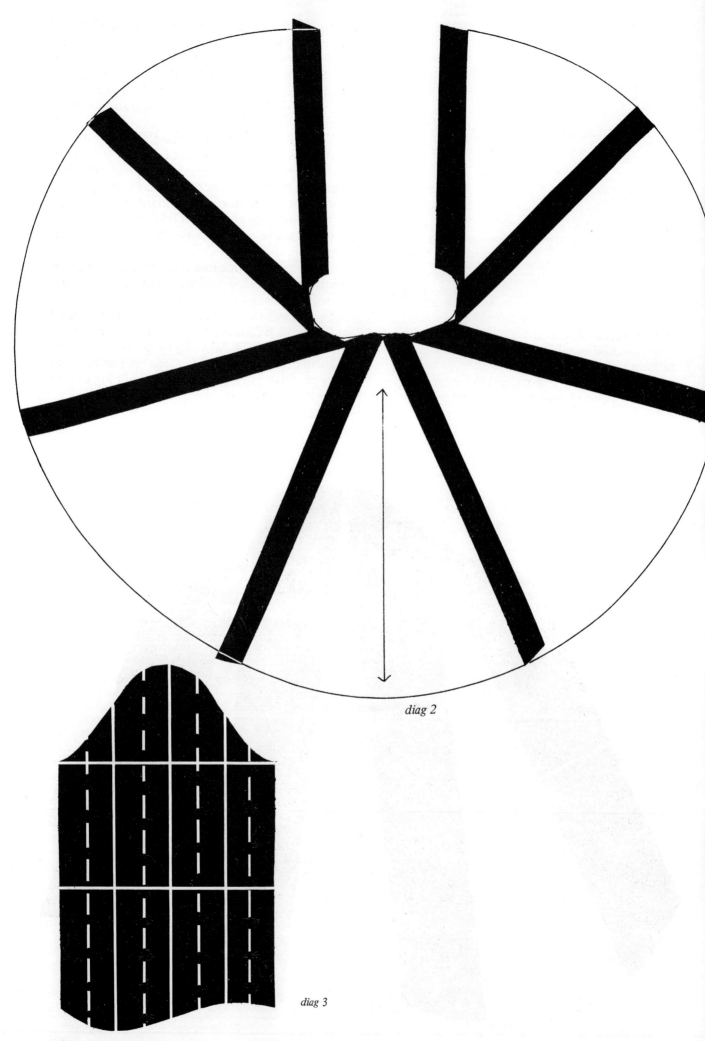

diag 2

diag 3

(52cm) should be added by this method (i.e. finished hem width approx 34" (88cm)). If more fullness is required method 2 should be used.

Outline the sleeve block and draw the new hem line as described on page 103. Cut along the hem line. Cut along the u/arm line (A-B) and then cut the lower part of the sleeve along the three construction lines from the hem to within $\frac{1}{8}$" (3mm) of the u/arm line, so that the four sections are just held together. Pin the s/h on to a new sheet of paper and continue the centre line down for the length of the sleeve. Place the lower sections so that the hem measures the required amount and the top of each side seam is touching the u/arm line. Add most width at the back arm line.

Correct the curve of the hem line and curve the side seams to A and B as shown.

Bishop sleeve—3

This method enables a fairly large amount of fullness to be added at the hem while retaining a close fitting s/h. However, no more than 20"

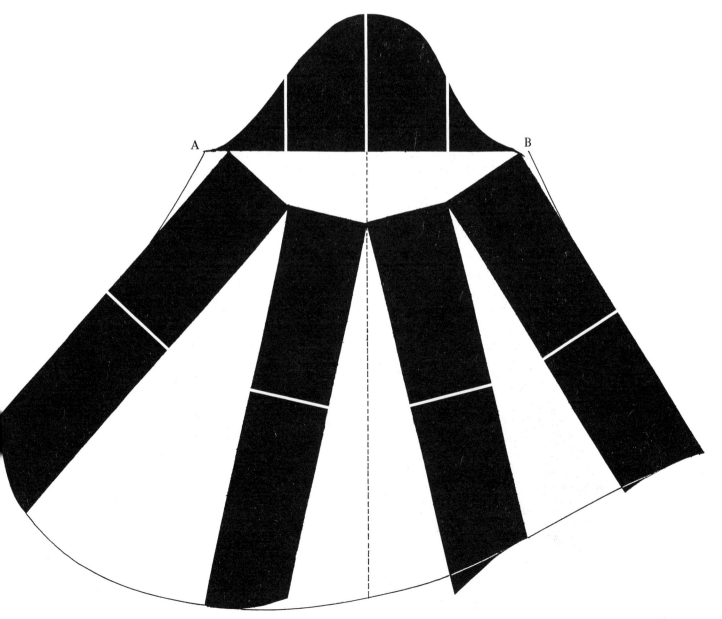

Cut along the hem line. Cut across the pattern on a line parallel to the u/arm line and 5"-6" (12.7cm-15.2cm) below it (A-B). Cut the lower section along the three construction lines from the hem to within $\frac{1}{8}$" (3mm) of the line A-B so that the sections just remain joined.

Pin the upper part of the sleeve on to a new sheet of paper and continue the centre line down for the length of the sleeve. Place the lower sections so that the hem line measures the required amount and the top of each side seam is touching the line A-B. No more than 10" (25cm) should be added when the sleeve is cut across at this level. The position of the line A-B may be varied according to the shape of sleeve required, which makes this the most versatile method. The cut may even be made on the elbow line or below, although the lower the cut, the less fullness may be added if the sleeve is to be a good shape. The side seams must always be curved very carefully and smoothly as this affects the shape of the finished sleeve.

Curve the side seams, by-passing points A and B, and correct the curve of the hem line.

Bishop sleeve—4

This method is used to obtain fullness at the wrist while retaining a narrow sleeve above the elbow.

Outline the sleeve block and draw the new hem line as described on page 103.

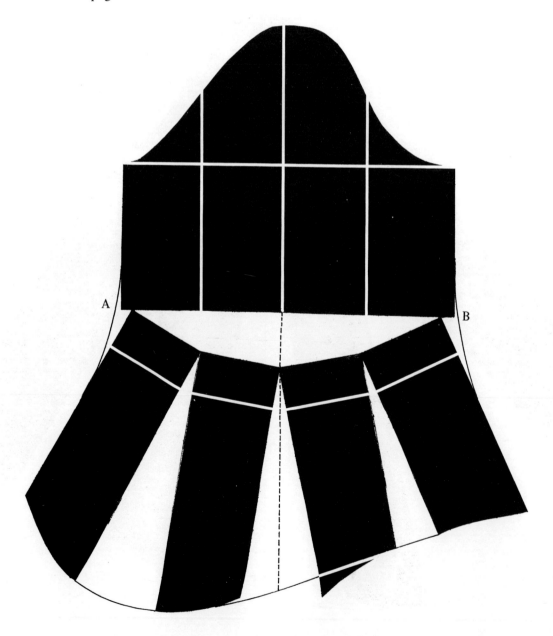

Bell Sleeves

Peasant Sleeves

Any of the four methods used to construct a bishop sleeve pattern may be used for a bell sleeve without, of course, subtracting any length to allow for a cuff or adding length for the sleeve to blouse over. However, since shape and hang are of paramount importance in a bell sleeve, the methods which use cutting and spreading to achieve fullness are to be preferred, i.e. methods 2 and 3. Method 4 is not advisable unless the sleeve is to be cut with a seam around the upper arm, in which case method 4 would be used but the pattern would remain in two parts.

Add an extra ½" (13mm) to the length on the back arm line to give a graceful curve to the hemline.

See page 110 for a puffed sleeve pattern which may also be used as a pattern for a short bell sleeve.

Peasant sleeves are full sleeves which are gathered in at the wrist by elastic.

Any of the four bishop sleeve methods may also be used for a peasant sleeve, the only difference being that extra length is added for the sleeve to blouse over at the wrist (page 103) but no length is subtracted to allow for a cuff.

Wrist Opening

Any sleeve which is gathered into a cuff must have an opening at the wrist. To find the position of the opening—divide the width of the pattern at the hem by three and measure this amount from the *back* side seam along the hem line, i.e. if the sleeve has a hem width of 18" (42.5cm) measure 6" (15.2cm) from the back side seam. The opening is usually 3"-4" (7.6cm-10.2cm) long and parallel to the straight grain line.

Raised Sleeveheads

This section includes puffed sleeves, which are traditionally short and may be gathered at the s/h, hem or both; Victorian sleeves, which are long, with fullness gathered into a cuff or elastic at the wrist and fullness gathered or pleated at the shoulder; Leg o'mutton sleeves, which are tight between wrist and elbow and very full at the top; and darted s/heads and set-in bands across the s/h, both of which give a square-shouldered effect.

Puffed sleeves

Puffed sleeves have fullness added between the front and back arm lines which is gathered into the a/h so that the sleeve stands out above and beyond the line of the arm. The back of the sleeve should have slightly more fullness than the front as the gathers are most effective at the back. The under part of the sleeve is set in without gathering, since gathers there would be bulky and uncomfortable to wear. It is usual for a puffed sleeve to be gathered both at the s/h and the hem, although it may be gathered in one position only.

The amount added between each of the sections is usually 1"-3" (2.5cm-7.6cm) but depends on the shape of sleeve required and the weight of the fabric—the lighter the weight, the more fullness can be gathered in.

Puffed sleeves must also have extra length added wherever width is added: at the s/h to allow the sleeve to stand up at the shoulder, and at the hem, particularly on the centre and back arm lines, to allow the sleeve to blouse over. Again the amount depends on fabric and personal preference, but an average amount is 2" (5.0cm).

Puffed sleeves are most effective when they are very short—the u/arm seam should not be longer than 2"-3" (5.0cm-7.6cm).

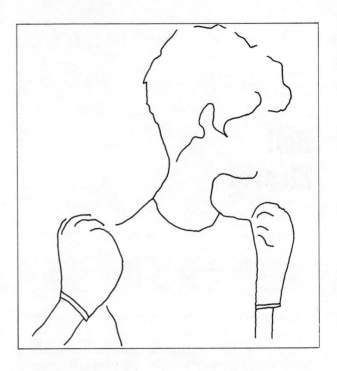

Puffed sleeve—1

Outline the sleeve block, cut across at the required length and divide the sleeve into sections as described on page 109. Cut along each of the lines and spread the sections apart at the s/h to obtain the fullness required, allowing slightly more fullness at the back. The sections may be overlapped at the hem (as shown) to obtain a close fitting hem. Add approx 2" (5.0cm) extra height on the centre line, curving into the original line at the balance marks and adding more height at the back arm line than the front.

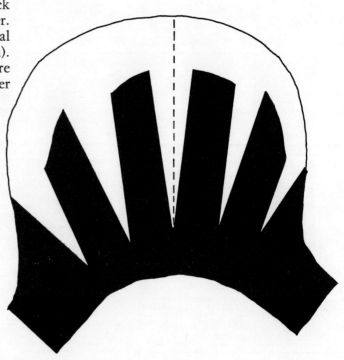

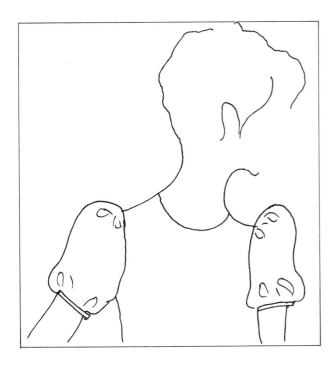

sleeve block is prepared in this way for each of the puffed sleeve methods. Number the sections before cutting to ensure that they remain in the same order when spread apart.

On a new sheet of paper, draw two lines crossing at right angles to represent the centre line and u/arm line of the new pattern. Cut along each of the five construction lines and spread the sections apart, adding 1"-3" (2.5cm-7.6cm) between the sections and keeping the u/arm line straight, as shown in diagram 2. The diagram shows the same amount of fullness added at s/h and hem but more may be added to one edge if required (the u/arm line would then be slightly curved—see diags on page 108 and 110).

Add extra length at the s/h, curving into the original at the balance points, and at the hem, curving into the original hemline near the side seams.

Puffed sleeve—2

Outline the sleeve block and cut across at the required length, parallel to the u/arm line. Draw two extra construction lines—one mid-way between the back arm line and the centre line (A-B), and one mid-way between the centre line and the front arm line (C-D) (see diag 1). The

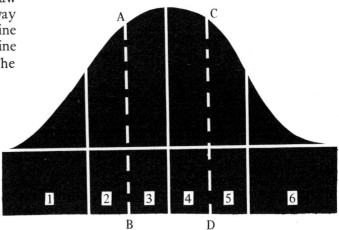

diag 1

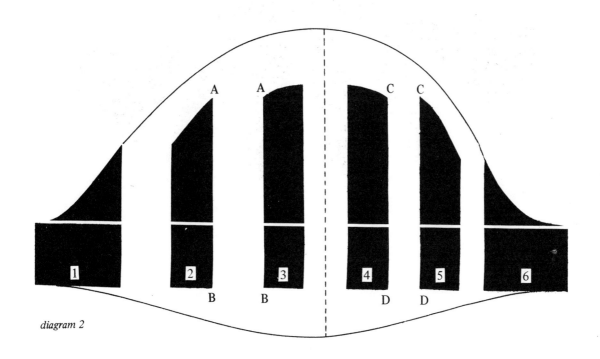

diagram 2

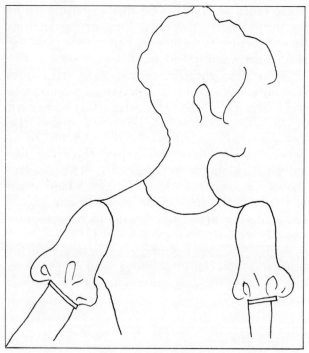

Puffed sleeve—3

Outline the sleeve block and cut across at the required length, parallel to the u/arm line. Draw the extra construction lines as described on page 109. Cut along the lines from the hem to within $\frac{1}{8}$" (3mm) of the s/h and spread the sections apart at the hem as required, allowing slightly more fullness at the back. Add approximately 2" (5.0cm) extra length to the hem on the centre line, curving into the original hemline near the side seams. (Add more length to the back arm line than the front arm line.)

Short bell sleeve

The pattern for this sleeve may be made by following the instructions for a puffed sleeve—method 2, but adding only ½" (13mm) extra length on the centre and back arm lines and curving smoothly into the original hemline.

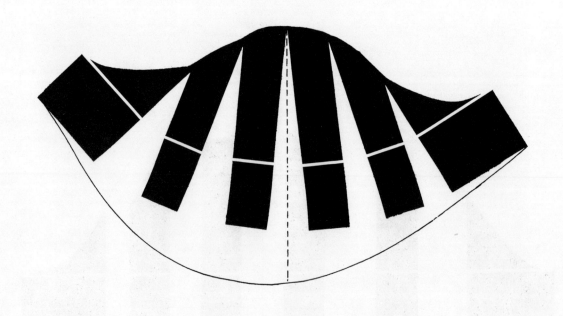

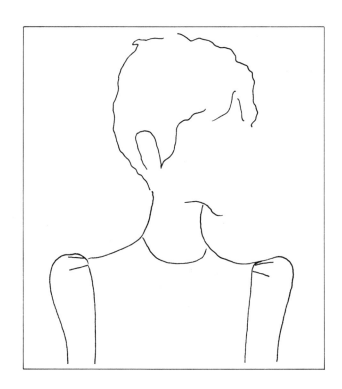

Darted sleevehead

Outline the sleeve block. Measure 1" (2.5cm) each side of the centre line (points A and B) and join to point C on the u/arm line (diag 1). Cut down the centre line and across the u/arm line to within $\frac{1}{8}$" (3mm) of the side seams. Cut from A and B to within $\frac{1}{8}$" (3mm) of C. Pin the lower part of the sleeve on to a new sheet of paper and continue the centre line upwards. Raise the sleevehead until the required amount of fullness has been added—usually 2"-4" (5.0cm-10.2cm) altogether. Divide the fullness equally between the three positions and draw the darts as shown in diag 2—1½"-2" (3.8cm-5.0cm) long.

If more than three darts are required further cuts may be made each side of A and B.

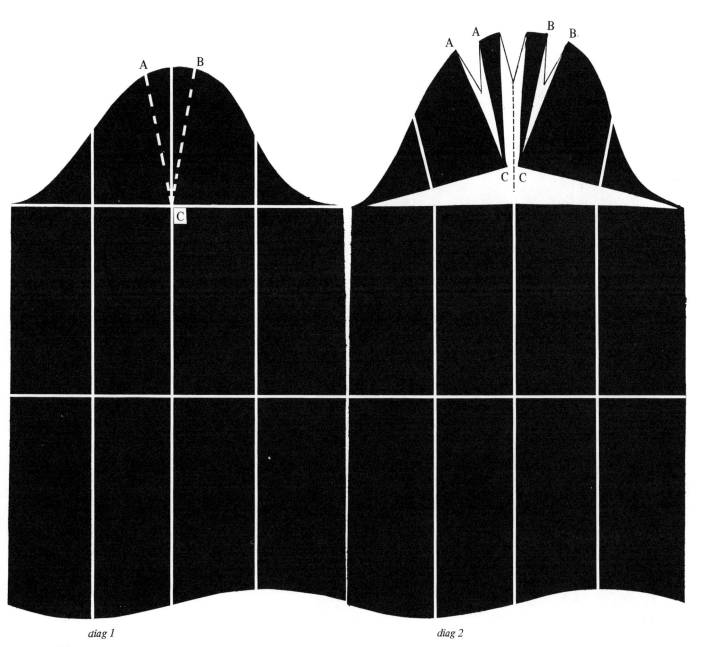

diag 1   diag 2

111

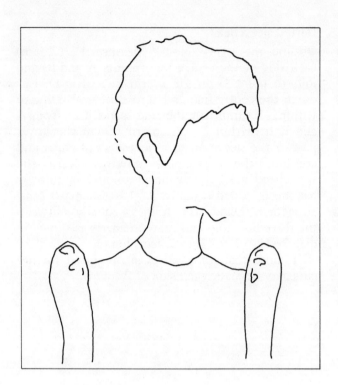

Gathered sleevehead—1

This method enables fullness to be added to the upper part of the s/h while keeping the lower part close fitting.

Outline the sleeve block.

Draw a line across 3" (7.6cm) below the top of the s/h and parallel to the u/arm line (A-B). Cut down the centre line and across the new line to within $\frac{1}{8}$" (3mm) of A and B. Pin the lower part of the sleeve pattern on to a new sheet of paper and continue the centre line upwards. Raise the s/h sections until the required amount of fullness has been added (not more than 4" (10.2cm)). Correct the line of the s/h as shown.

The method shown on the previous page for a darted s/h may also be used for a gathered s/h if more fullness is required or if the fullness is required to spring from the u/arm line.

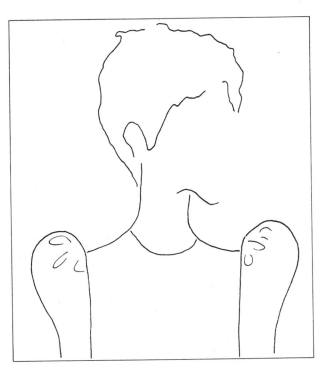

Gathered sleevehead—2

This is an alternative method to that shown on the previous two pages and enables more fullness to be added.

Outline the sleeve block.

Draw a line across 3" (7.6cm) below the s/h, parallel to the u/arm line, (line A-B). Cut down the centre line and across the u/arm line to within $\frac{1}{8}$" (3mm) of the side seams. Cut across the new line to within $\frac{1}{8}$" (3mm) of points A and B.

Pin the lower part of the sleeve on to a new sheet of paper and continue the centre line upwards. Raise the four sections until the required amount of fullness has been added (not more than 10" (25cm)). Correct the line of the s/h as shown.

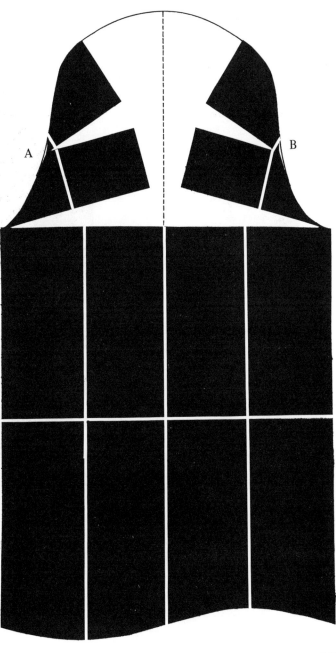

Draw a line across the pattern 1"-2" (2.5cm-5.0cm) above the elbow line (line A-B) and a second line 3" (7.6cm) below the u/arm line, (line C-D). Mark points E and F where the back and front arm lines meet the line C-D (diag 1).

Cut across the line A-B. Pin the lower part of the sleeve on to a new sheet of paper and continue the centre line upwards for approx 20" (52cm). On the upper part of the sleeve—cut through the centre line and across to within $\frac{1}{8}$" (3mm) of points C and D; cut from the s/h along the back arm line and front arm line to within $\frac{1}{8}$" (3mm) of points E and F.

Place the upper part of the sleeve with points A and B touching the line A-B on the lower part and raise the six sections until the required amount of fullness has been added. (The diagram shows 30" (78cm) added). Correct the curves of the side seams. Add 4"-5" (10.2cm-12.5cm) extra height to the s/h and draw the new s/h curve as shown, curving smoothly into the original s/h at back and front arm lines.

Leg o'mutton sleeve

A leg o'mutton sleeve is tight fitting between elbow and wrist but very full at the top, with the fullness gathered or pleated into the a/h. An opening would be needed at the wrist, either along the back arm line or in the side seam.

Outline the sleeve block and adapt it to a tight fitting sleeve as shown on page 97.

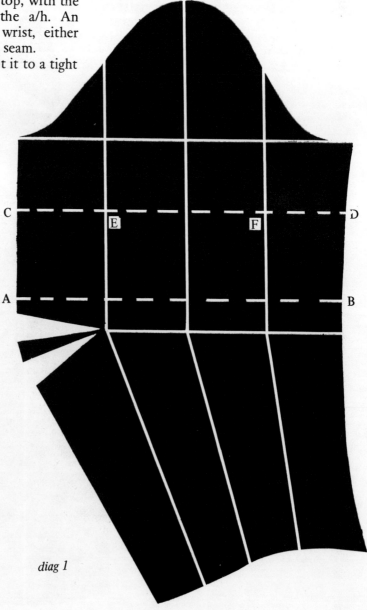

diag 1

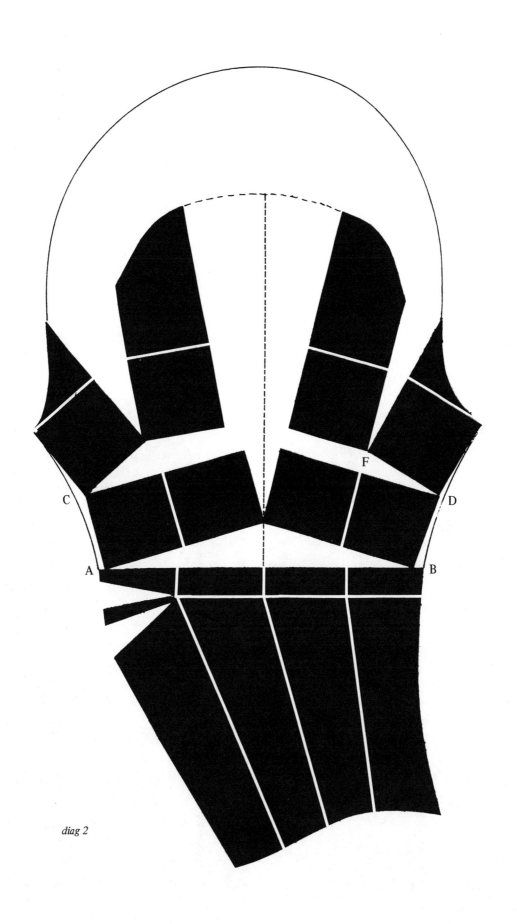

diag 2

115

Sleeve with inset band

The adaptations shown on this and the following two pages are used to give a square shouldered effect.

Outline the sleeve block. Draw a line across the s/h parallel to the u/arm line and 4" (10.2cm) above it (line A-B). Cut down the centre line and across the u/arm line to within $\frac{1}{8}$" (3mm) of the side seams. Pin the lower part of the sleeve on to a new sheet of paper and continue the centre line upwards. Raise the s/h sections approximately 1" (2.5cm).

Draw a 1" (2.5cm) band around the top of the s/h with the ends of the band squared out from points A and B, (diag 1).

Cut the band away (diag 2), measure the *lower* edge and cut a straight strip of that length, 1" (2.5cm) wide (diag 3).

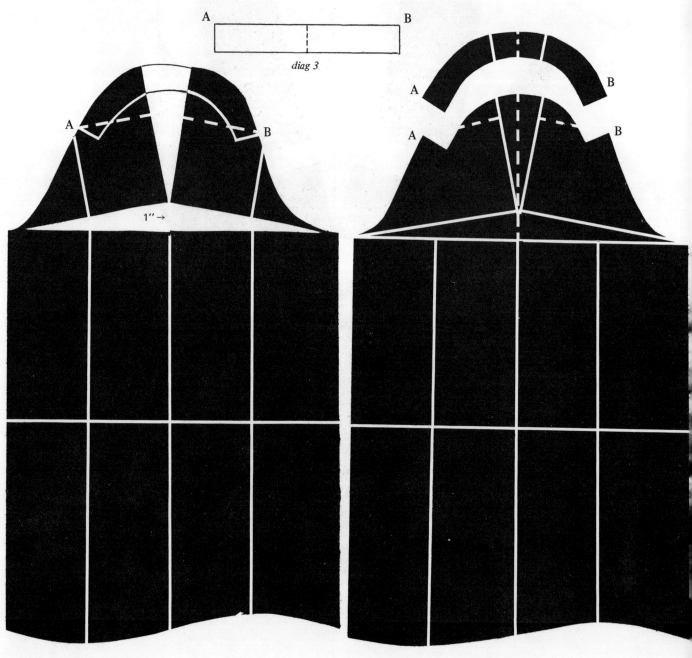

diag 3

diag 1

diag 2

Sleeve head with joined inset band

Outline the sleeve block. Draw the line A-B parallel to the u/arm line and 3" (7.6cm) above it. Draw a 1" (2.5cm) band around the top of the s/h with the ends of the band squared out from points A and B.

Cut down the centre line for 1" (2.5cm) and along the inner curve of the band, but not across the ends. Snip from the inner curve every ½" (13mm) almost to the outer edge and raise the bands until the edges are straight (diag 1). Cut along the centre line as far as the u/arm line and across the u/arm line to within $\frac{1}{8}$" (3mm) of the side seams. Raise the s/h until the curve C-D is ½" (13mm) greater than the inner edges of the bands—C-E plus D-F (diag 2).

diag 1   *diag 2*

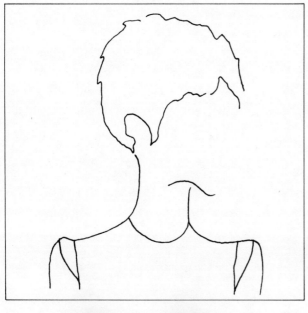

Sleeve head with curved inset band

This sleeve has a crescent shaped band over the shoulder.

Outline the sleeve block and draw the line A-B parallel to the u/arm line and 3" (7.6cm) above it. Cut down the centre line and across the u/arm line. Raise the s/h 1½" (3.8cm).

Mark a point 1½" (3.8cm) down from the new s/h on the centre line (point C) and curve from C to A and B (diag 1).

Cut the curved band away, as shown on diag 2, and cut into the *longer* edge at ½" (13mm) intervals. Overlap the cut edges until the crescent shape is reversed (diag 3) and the m/ment of the new s/h—that is, D-A plus B-E plus the upper edge of the crescent in diag 3—is equal to the s/h of the original block.

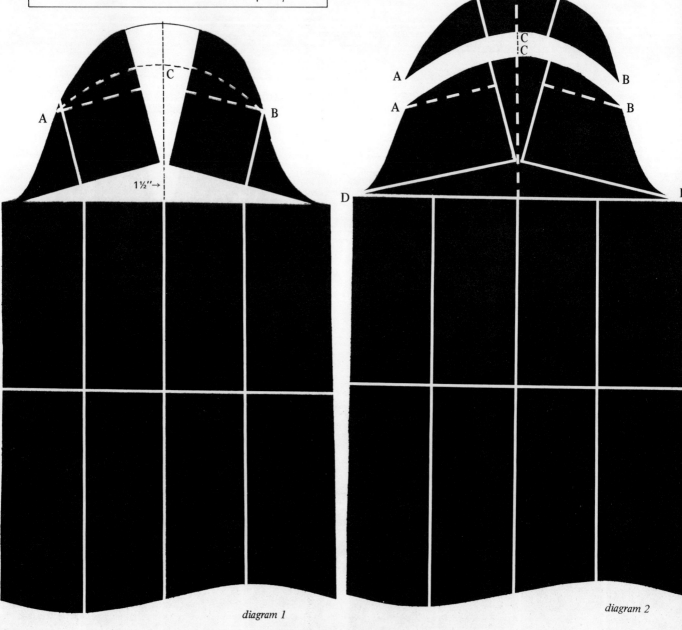

diagram 1

diagram 2

diagram 3

118

Long Frilled Sleeve

Decide on the depth of frill (usually 2"-3" (5.0cm-7.6cm)) and cut a rectangle of paper (A-B-C-D) measuring the width of the sleeve pattern at the wrist by the depth of frill required (diag 2). Cut into one of the long edges of the rectangle at ½" (13mm) intervals almost to the other edge and spread the sections apart until they form a circle, remembering to leave at least ½" (13mm) between the two short edges for the seam allowance (diag 3). Draw a smooth curve around the outer edge.

To make a short frilled sleeve—adapt the block to a short sleeve as shown on page 99, then proceed as above.

Adapt the sleeve block to a tight fitting sleeve as shown on page 97. (See diag 1). An opening will be needed at the wrist and should be made in the side seam.

diag 2

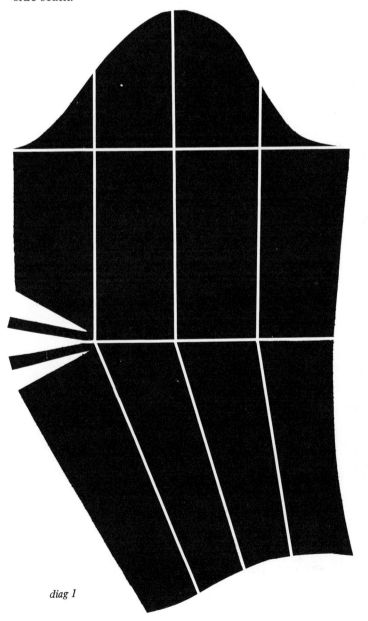

diag 1

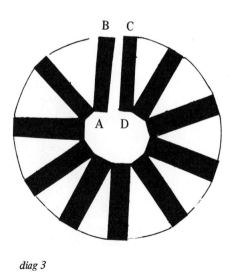

diag 3

Shallow Sleevehead

This adaptation may be used for sportswear, mens' shirts, uniforms and children's wear. It is intended to give additional freedom of movement but does not give an attractive appearance as it invariably pulls and creases from the shoulder bone. It should only be used when freedom of movement is more important than good fit. Making the s/h shallower causes the upper part of the sleeve to stand away from the arm so that upward movements are not restricted and the s/h is also made slightly wider between the balance points for the same reason. This adaptation is only suitable for short (above elbow) sleeves.

Outline the sleeve block and cut across at the required length. Draw curved lines from the u/arm points (A and B) to the top of the s/head (C), passing approximately 1" (2.5cm) from the balance points (D and E) (diag 1).

Cut along the curved lines from A and B to within $\frac{1}{8}$" (3mm) of C, and snip from the curve to within $\frac{1}{8}$" (3mm) of D and E.

Pin the lower part of the sleeve on to a new sheet of paper and draw the new u/arm line 1½"-2" (3.8cm-5.0cm) above the existing line (line F-G). Raise points A and B on to the line F-G. The side seams are usually drawn straight down from A and B to give additional width at the hem.

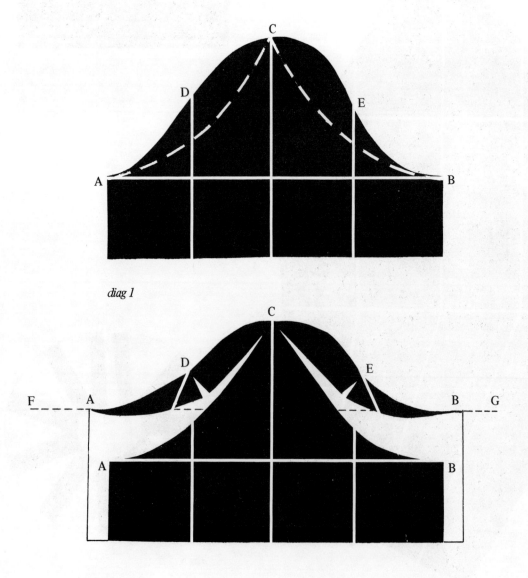

diag 1

diag 2

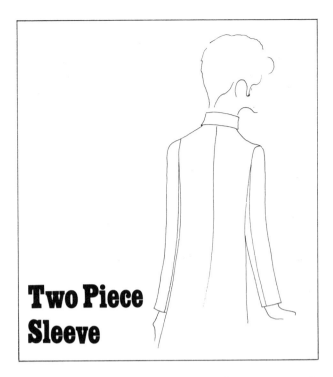

Two Piece Sleeve

In the two-piece sleeve the normal u/arm seam is moved forward and an additional seam is made at the back of the arm, passing over the elbow point. This sleeve is used in coats and jackets and occasionally in tailored dresses. The two seams enable the sleeve to fit closely but, because the sections are shaped to fit the curve of the arm, there is still sufficient ease for movement. The under section is sometimes cut on the bias grain for additional ease.

Outline the sleeve block and cut it out. Fold the sides under along the back arm line and front arm line (diag 1). Calculate the desired width at the wrist (minimum 9"-10" (22.4cm-25cm) for a coat or jacket). Measure half that amount along the wrist line from the front arm line towards the back arm line and mark point A. Join A to the elbow point and cut along that line through double paper.

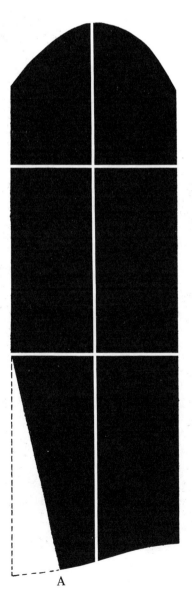

diag 1

Diag 2

Open out the sleeve. Measure 1½" (3.8cm) from the front arm line towards the side seam and draw a parallel line (line B-C). Cut the pattern along the line B-C and move the u/arm section to the other side of the pattern so that the original side seams are together (diag 3).

Measure ½" (13mm) from the back balance point towards the u/arm (point D). Join D to the elbow point. This line will form the back seam of the sleeve.

Diag 4

Fold the pattern in half lengthways. Calculate the desired width at the elbow (minimum 13" (33cm) in a coat or jacket) and measure half that amount along the elbow line, from the fold. Mark point E. Curve from E to the s/h and wrist and cut through double paper.

Diag 5

Cut from D to the elbow point to separate the two parts of the sleeve. Curve smoothly around the elbow point on both parts.

Diag 6

Cut the upper sleeve from the elbow point to within $\frac{1}{8}$" (3mm) of the front seam. Open ½" (13mm) at the elbow point. This amount is eased in when the sleeve is made up and provides a little extra fabric over the elbow to prevent the sleeve riding up.

Mark the straight grain line parallel to the centre line above the elbow line as shown. The straight grain line of the under sleeve is parallel to the original side seam. (See diag 5—broken line.)

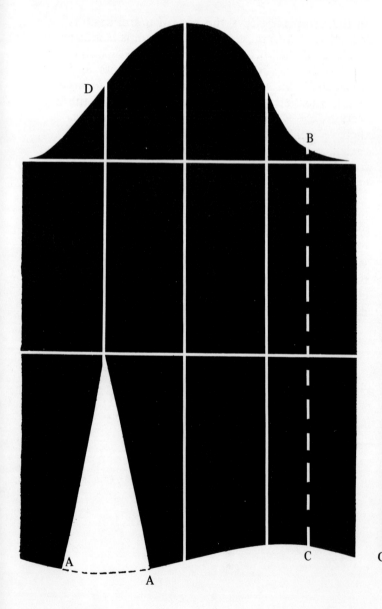

diag 2

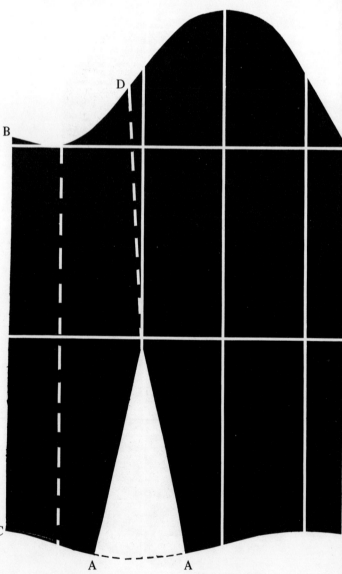

diag 3

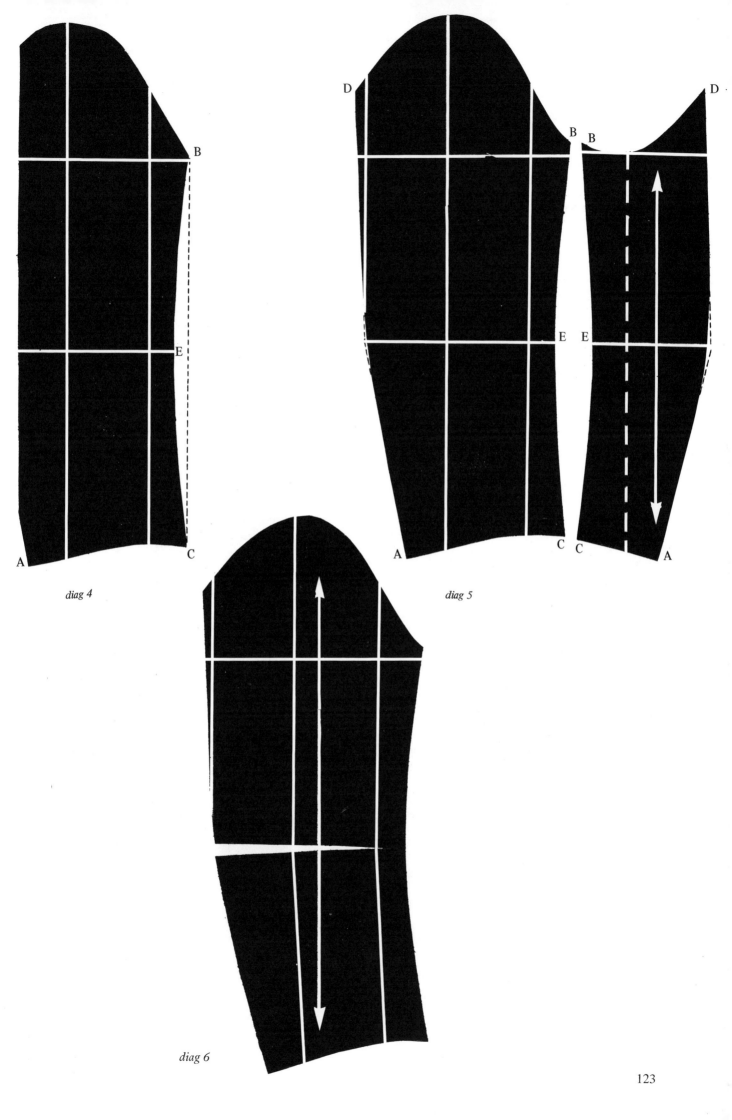

diag 4

diag 5

diag 6

123

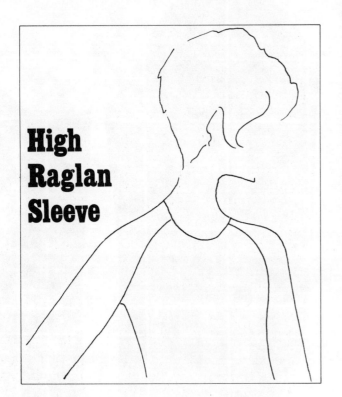

High Raglan Sleeve

by the ease at the top of the s/h.) Keep the points C and D as close as possible to the s/h, if necessary overlapping the raglan section and the s/h. (The diagram shows the front section overlapping slightly.) The curved edges of the sleeve—E-C-A and F-D-B—should measure approximately ½" (13mm) more than the corresponding edges of the bodice—A-C-G and B-D-H—and this amount is eased in between A-C or B-D. Correct the curved edges of the sleeve carefully around C and D (diag 3).

Mark a point approx. 3" (7.6cm) below the s/h (J). Curve from J, bypassing the shoulder points, to the neck points for the shoulder dart. The dart must extend below the original s/h to give a smooth curve over the shoulder bone.

High raglan sleeve

This type of raglan is normally used for dresses and the low raglan and deep raglan for coats and jackets. The shoulder seam *must* be centralised for all raglan adaptations and it may even be advisable to bring the seam ½" (13mm) further forward to counteract the tendency of a raglan sleeve to slip back, especially if the figure has rounded shoulders.

Bodice

Centralize the shoulder seam. Draw the raglan style lines on the back and front bodices. The basic raglan line curves from 1" (2.5cm) below the new neck points (A and B) to approximately 2" (5.0cm) below the balance points (C and D), although this may be varied according to individual preference. However, the line must always curve upwards slightly between the neck line and the balance point as this gives a more flattering effect, and it must curve very smoothly into the a/h at C and D. Make a balance mark on each of the raglan seams close to the neckline as shown and then cut along the raglan lines. Name the front and back sections and name the shoulder seam on each as they are not easily recognizable when cut away. The back shoulder dart should be folded out in the raglan section (dart position shown as broken line in diag 2). The dart remaining in the bodice is sufficiently narrow to be eased in.

Sleeve

Outline the sleeve block and continue the centre line upwards for approximately 6" (15.2cm).

Place the raglan sections to the s/h so that the shoulder points are ½"-1" (13mm-2.5cm) apart and approximately ½" (13mm) above the s/h. (This ½" (13mm) allows ease over the shoulder bone which, in an inset sleeve, would be provided

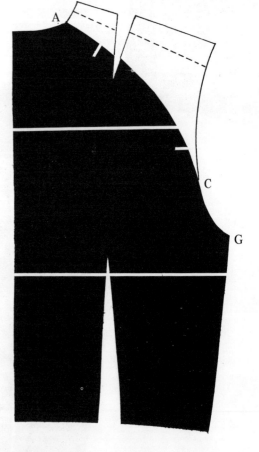

diag 1

diag 2

diag 3

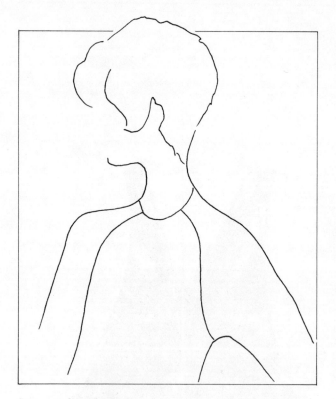

Low raglan sleeve

This sleeve is cut lower under the arm than the previous sleeve and for that reason is often used on coats as it enables bulky clothes to be worn underneath.

Bodice

Centralize the shoulder and side seams. Draw the raglan style lines—usually curving from 1"-2" (2.5cm-5.0cm) below the new neck points (A and B)

to approximately 2" (5.0cm) below the u/arm points (C and D). It is important to the finished effect that the line curves up slightly near the neck line, as shown. Place the side seams together to ensure that the curve is smooth and continuous across the seam. Make balance marks across the raglan line—one near to the neck line (E) and one near the side seam (F). Name the front and back raglan sections, name the shoulder seam on each and cut along the raglan lines. Fold out the back shoulder dart on the raglan section.

Sleeve

Outline the sleeve block and continue the centre line upwards for approximately 6" (15.2cm).

From the a/h edges of the raglan sections clip to within $\frac{1}{8}$" (3mm) of the raglan curves at $\frac{1}{2}$" (13mm) intervals and at right angles to the a/h. Clip between u/arm and balance points only.

Place the raglan sections to the s/h with the shoulder points $\frac{1}{2}$"-1" (13mm-2.5cm) apart and $\frac{1}{2}$"-1" (13mm-2.5cm) above the s/h. Keeping the a/h as close as possible to the s/h, spread the raglan sections apart until they fit to the curve of the a/h, as shown. Correct the sleeve seams, curving them into the original seams at the elbow line.

Mark a point 3" (7.6cm) down from the s/h (E) and curve from E to the neck points, bypassing the shoulder points. The sleeve may be cut in two sections by cutting along the edges of the dart to E and along the centre line of the sleeve.

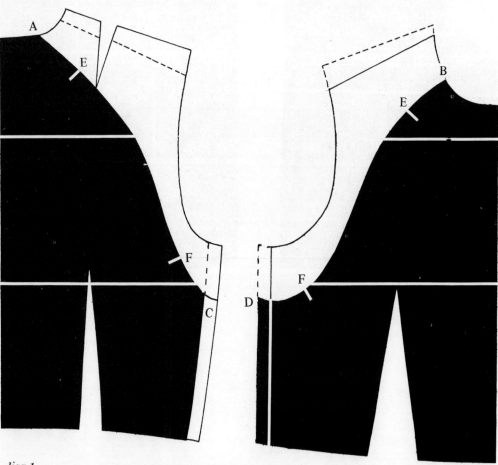

diag 1

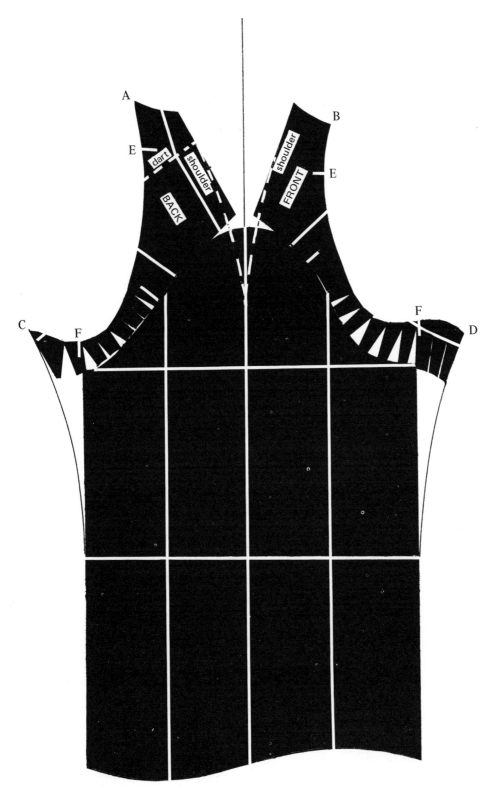

diag 2

Deep raglan sleeve
The third type of raglan is simply a kimono sleeve with a raglan style line added. It is very similar in appearance to the low raglan, although slightly looser fitting, and the pattern is made by drawing a style line, as for the low raglan, on the kimono block (see page 136).

The block is then cut along the raglan line and along the gusset line as far as the balance point, and the sections spread apart to incorporate a gusset as in the low drop-shoulder on page

High drop shoulder
The drop shoulder cut follows the same principle as the raglan, but in reverse: a section of the sleeve pattern is cut away and joined to the bodice pattern. As with the raglan cut, there are two types of drop shoulder—the high drop shoulder, which has a style line crossing the original a/h at or near the balance points and which therefore fits as closely under the arm as a set-in sleeve; and the low drop shoulder which has a lower style line and can most conveniently be cut on the kimono block. The low drop shoulder is looser fitting, as is any style cut on the kimono block.

Sleeve
Measure 4" (10.2cm) down on the centre line, or as required (point A).

Square across from the front balance point (B) to C on the back s/h. Curve from C through A to B and cut along that line. On the s/h section measure up ½" (13mm) from B and C (D and E) and curve a new line D-A-E. Cut along that line. (This is to remove some of the ease which is included in the s/h.) Cut the s/h section along the centre line (A-F) and name the front and back sections.

Bodice
Centralise the shoulder seams. Raise the shoulder points ½" (13mm) (G and H) and connect to the neck points.
Place the s/h sections to the a/h with point F on each section ½" (13mm) from point G or H and a ¼" (6mm) gap at points E and F. (It may be necessary to overlap the s/h section and the bodice slightly, especially at the front.)

Curve the new shoulder seams as shown, bypassing F, G and H, to obtain a smooth curve

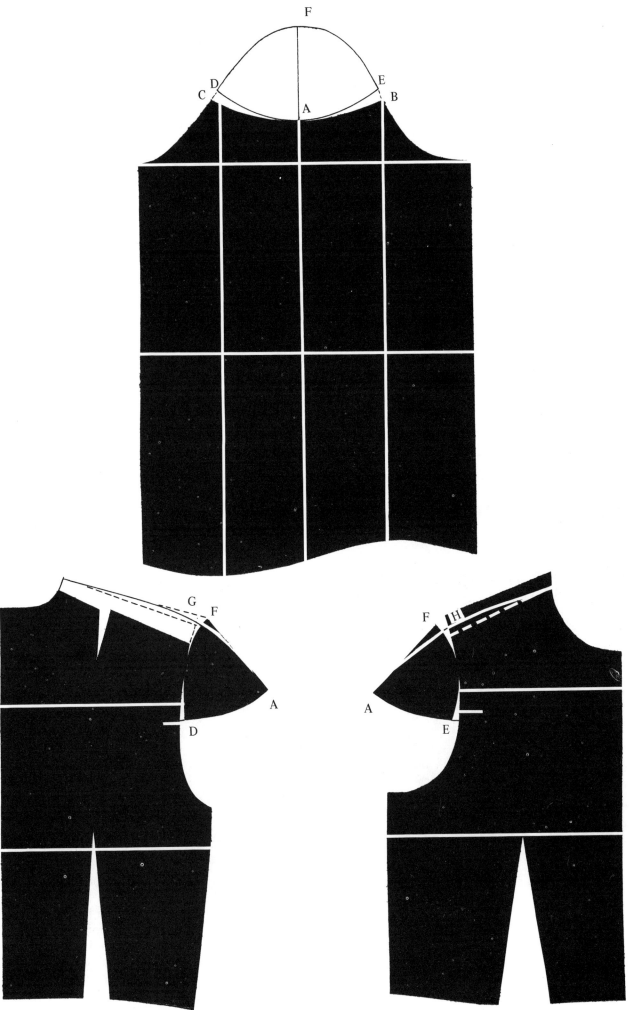

to point B which is on the gusset line, 2"-3" (5.0cm-7.6cm) above the u/arm point, C. The line should be at right angles to the overarm seam at A and at right angles to the gusset line at B. Cut along the line A-B-C. Measure ½" (13mm) from C along the sleeve seam (D) and join D-B. Cut from D to within $\frac{1}{8}$" (3mm) of B and spread the sections until approximately 2½" (6.3cm) has been added. This takes the place of a gusset but is neater than a gusset since it is incorporated in the style seam and thus invisible. Correct the sleeve seam by curving from C to the elbow line as shown.

Make the front pattern in the same way.

Low drop shoulder

Outline the back kimono block. (See page 136.) Measure 10"-14" (25cm-35.2cm) along the overarm seam from the neck point (A). Curve from A

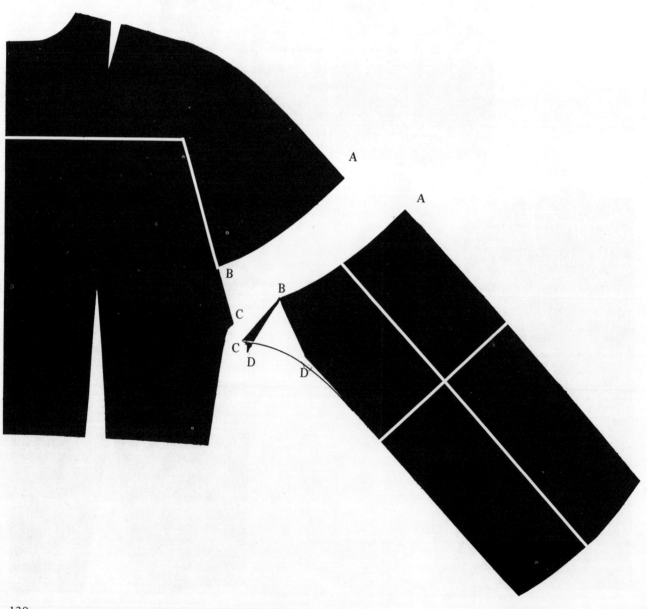

Square Armhole-1

A square a/h may be cut from the bodice and sleeve blocks or it may be cut from a kimono block, depending on the effect required. (The former will be higher and closer fitting under the arm.)

This method uses the bodice and sleeve blocks.

Bodice
Outline the back bodice block and centralize the side seam.

Draw a straight line from the back shoulder point (A) through the back balance point (B), continuing to bust level. Measure down 1" (2.5cm) from the u/arm point (C) to point D. Square across from the line A-B to D. Mark point E where the lines cross. Cut the u/arm section away along the line B-E-D. Cut into the u/arm section at ½" (13mm) intervals from the a/h edge to within $\frac{1}{8}$" (3mm) of the line B-E-D.

Sleeve
Outline the sleeve block. Place point B of the u/arm section to the back balance point and spread the sections apart, keeping the line B-C as close as possible to the s/h. Extend the u/arm line of the sleeve as a guide line and spread the sections around until point C is on that line. Curve the new sleeve seam from D into the original seam at elbow level.

Make the front pattern in the same way.

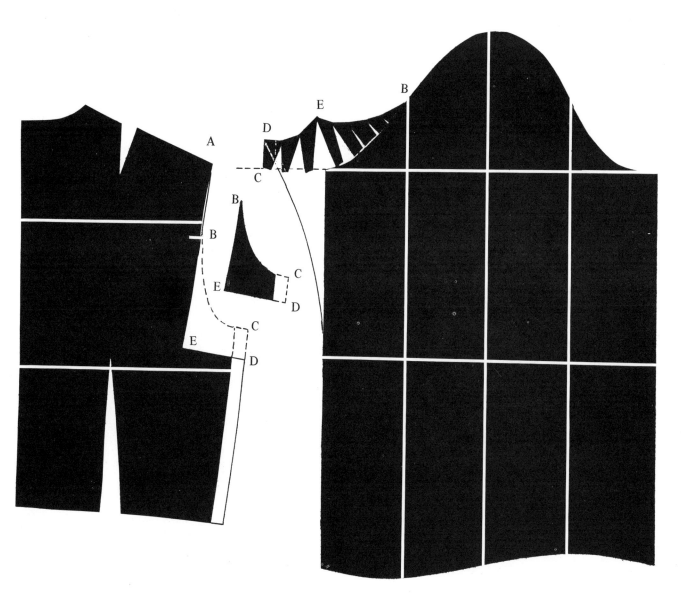

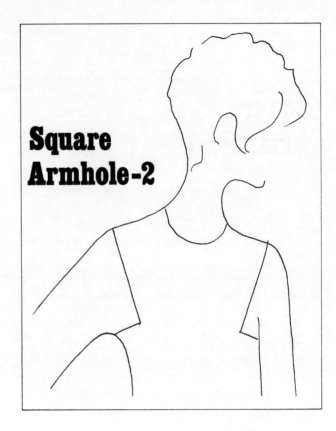

Square Armhole-2

This style is cut on the kimono block (see page 136).

Outline the back kimono block.

Draw a straight line from the shoulder point (A) through the balance point (B) continuing to bust level, as in the previous adaptation. Square across from the line A-B to the u/arm point (C). Mark point D where the lines cross. Cut along the line A-B-C-D to separate bodice and sleeve.

Sleeve

Cut along the line C-B (which is the gusset line) to within $\frac{1}{8}$" (3mm) of B. Cut from the line B-C into the line B-D at ½" (13mm) intervals as shown, and spread the sections apart until 4"-5" (10.2cm-12.6cm) has been added at point C. This replaces most of the u/arm length which was lost in the making of the kimono block and is thus a concealed gusset. The hollowing of the curve B-D imitates the shape of the lower part of the sleeve block and gives a better fit to the u/arm area of this style. Correct the curve of the sleeve seam from C to the elbow line.

Make the front pattern in the same way, adding *exactly* the same amount at C for the gusset.

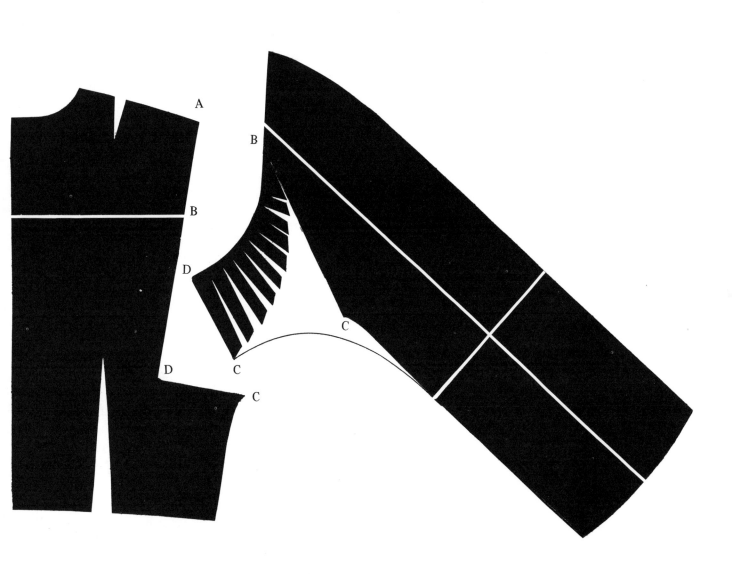

Deep Armhole

This adaptation enables the depth of the a/h to be increased without the considerable loss of u/arm length which would occur if the a/h and s/h were simply cut lower. (The problem of loss of u/arm length is explained in the kimono section, page 136.) Coats and jackets are often cut in this way as bulky clothes may then be worn underneath, although the appearance is that of a normal set-in sleeve.

A deep a/h may be cut from the bodice and sleeve blocks, as shown on this page, or from the kimono block following the principles used in cutting the low drop shoulder or the square a/h from kimono blocks (pages 130 and 132).

Bodice
Outline the bodice blocks and centralize the side seams. Mark the new u/arm points (A), usually 2"-4" (5.0cm-10.2cm) below the original u/arm points (B). Mark points C, ½" (13mm) in from each balance point. Curve from A to C and continue to the shoulder points (D) for the new a/h line. (Place the side seams together to ensure that the new a/h curve is continuous across the side seam.) Cut each a/h section away along the line A-C-D. Clip the sections from the original a/h to within $\frac{1}{8}$" (3mm) of the curve A-C-D at ½" (13mm) intervals.

Sleeve
Outline the sleeve block and extend the u/arm line each side.

Place the a/h sections to the s/h with shoulder points (D) meeting at the centre of the s/h, and spread the sections around keeping the edges close to the s/h until points B are on the extended u/arm line. Curve the new sleeve seams from A to the elbow line as shown, bypassing B.

This method also adds extra width to the u/arm line of the sleeve, which is desirable in a coat pattern.

Make the front pattern in the same way, ensuring that the sleeve seams are equal in length.

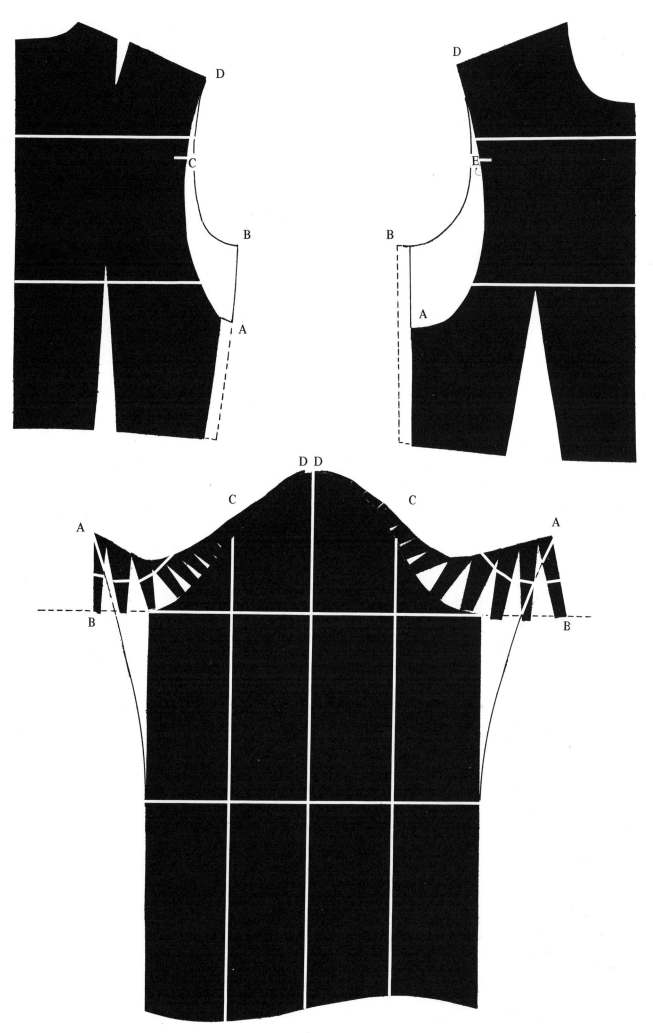

Kimono Sleeve

Definitions

The term 'Kimono' will be used as a general term to denote any type of sleeve which is cut in one piece with the bodice. There are various terms used to describe this type of cutting, such as dolman, bat-wing, magyar, etc. and since there are no standard definitions of these terms, the definitions to be used are as follows:

Kimono Used to describe a fairly close fitting sleeve with a gusset; and also as a general term to cover all sleeves which are cut in one piece with the bodice;

Bat-wing or dolman A looser, lower cut sleeve than the kimono. There is no gusset as the pattern is cut and spread apart to incorporate the extra u/arm length which a gusset would otherwise provide.

Magyar A very short kimono sleeve, just covering the shoulder, usually without a gusset. Also known as a cap sleeve.

A kimono sleeve gives an attractive continuous appearance to the bodice and sleeve, but is more difficult to cut than set-in sleeves if it is to be comfortable to wear, as there are many factors to take into account. Since there is no seam passing around the under-arm, the extra length which is needed in that area to enable the arm to be raised usually has to be added in the form of a gusset. Although sleeves which are very short or cut very low under the arm may not need a gusset. A separate set-in sleeve is able to adjust itself to all arm positions due to the seam passing around the arm, and the gusset in a kimono sleeve is a substitute for the u/arm seam.

The simplest and original kimono sleeve is that in which the shoulder seam is at right angles to the c/b and c/f (diag 1) and this is still the simplest way to cut a garment with sleeves, although the result will be very loose with many drapes and folds. However, it is obvious that this sleeve will fit best when the arms are raised and when the arms are lowered it would pull from the shoulder bone and feel tight, with bulky folds of material under the arm. This type of cutting is used in babywear, nightwear and loose fitting leisure garments.

It is, however, possible to cut a kimono sleeve which approaches the fit of a set-in sleeve while retaining the flattering line of the continuous bodice and sleeve: by pinning the sleeve at the shoulder point and pivoting it until it overlaps the bodice side seam. The shape shown in diag 2 should fit well when the arms were lowered but the length of the u/arm seam has been so reduced that it would be very difficult for the arms to be raised unless the lost u/arm length is replaced by a gusset. (The amount of length lost may be found by measuring from the new u/arm point (A) to the bodice u/arm point (B) plus from A to the sleeve u/arm point (C)—in this case 13½" (36cm).) Since the maximum width of a gusset is approximately 5" (10.2cm), it is obvious that this sleeve would not be successful.

Diags 1 and 2 show the two extremes in kimono shaping and, since neither fits well, the ideal kimono shape is to be found between the two. Although the u/arm length has been so much reduced in diag 2, the overarm length has remained the same, and it is the relationship between overarm and u/arm length which is the basis of kimono cutting. This principle will be better understood if the reader experiments with kimono cutting by pinning the s/h ½" (13mm) above the shoulder point (centralize the shoulder seam and cut the sleeve along the centre line first) and dropping the sleeve varying amounts to find the amount of u/arm length lost in each case. The more the sleeve overlaps the bodice, the more length is lost, but it should not overlap by more than 1½" (3.8cm) as this causes approximately 6" (12.7cm) to be lost, most of which can be replaced by the gusset. (If knitted fabric is to be used, the overlap may be increased to 2" (5.0cm).) (The overlap in diag 2 is 3½" (8.9cm).)

The problem in kimono cutting is therefore that the sleeve must be slanted sufficiently for it to fit well over the top of the arm without pulling from the shoulder bone, yet must not be slanted so far that more u/arm length is lost than can be replaced by a gusset.

Kimono designing

A kimono sleeve may be completely plain, with a separate diamond-shaped gusset added to the u/arm seam and the bust shaping introduced by means of a waist or u/arm dart, or the gusset may be incorporated into the design of the garment in a variety of ways (see pages 140-144). The method chosen depends on the effect required, for instance if a continuous bodice and sleeve with no visible seaming is desired, a standard diamond shaped gusset may be used (page 139). This is effective in replacing most of the lost u/arm length but there is a great deal of strain on the extreme point of the gusset which may cause it to tear, and it is very difficult to repair the point of a gusset due to the constant strain on it. Incorporating the gusset in a seam may solve the problem, although any seam in which there is a point (see pages 143, 144) will have the same problems as the diamond shaped gusset, and a gusset incorporated in a curved seam may be preferable,

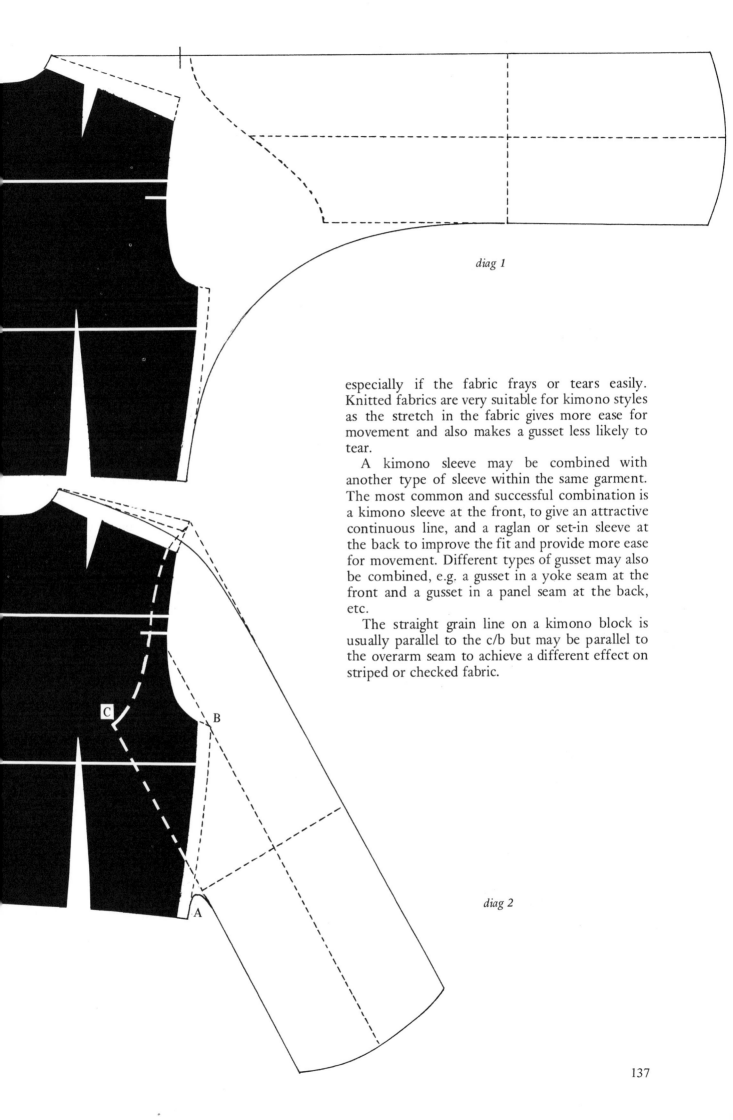

diag 1

especially if the fabric frays or tears easily. Knitted fabrics are very suitable for kimono styles as the stretch in the fabric gives more ease for movement and also makes a gusset less likely to tear.

A kimono sleeve may be combined with another type of sleeve within the same garment. The most common and successful combination is a kimono sleeve at the front, to give an attractive continuous line, and a raglan or set-in sleeve at the back to improve the fit and provide more ease for movement. Different types of gusset may also be combined, e.g. a gusset in a yoke seam at the front and a gusset in a panel seam at the back, etc.

The straight grain line on a kimono block is usually parallel to the c/b but may be parallel to the overarm seam to achieve a different effect on striped or checked fabric.

diag 2

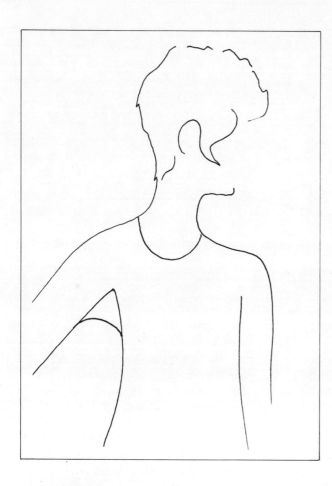

Kimono block

The kimono block must always be used with a gusset, which replaces the u/arm length lost when the bodice and sleeve are overlapped.

Outline the back bodice block and centralize the shoulder seam. (This is to ensure that the over-arm seam of the kimono sleeve, which is a continuation of the shoulder seam, passes along the centre of the arm.) It is also necessary to centralize the side seam, as bodice and sleeve seams join to become one seam in the kimono block.

Raise the shoulder point ½" (13mm) (point A) and connect to the neck point.

Place the top of the s/h (B) ½" (13mm) from A and swing the sleeve until the u/arm point (C) overlaps the side seam by approximately 1½" (3.8cm). Outline the sleeve, drawing all construction lines. Curve the shoulder seam, by-passing A and B, and draw the new shoulder dart, making it the same width on the new shoulder seam as on the original. Curve the side seam, by-passing point D which is the point where bodice and sleeve seams cross.

Make the front kimono block in the same way, except that the sleeve must overlap the bodice side seam slightly more than 1½" (3.8cm) to achieve the same slant. Place the blocks together to check that the slant of each is the same and check that the over-arm and u/arm seams match in length.

The gusset line, which shows the usual position for the gusset, is found as follows: join point D to the back or front balance point, then extend the line to meet the new u/arm seam (E). Measure 3"-4" (7.6cm-10.2cm) from E for the length of the gusset and mark point F.

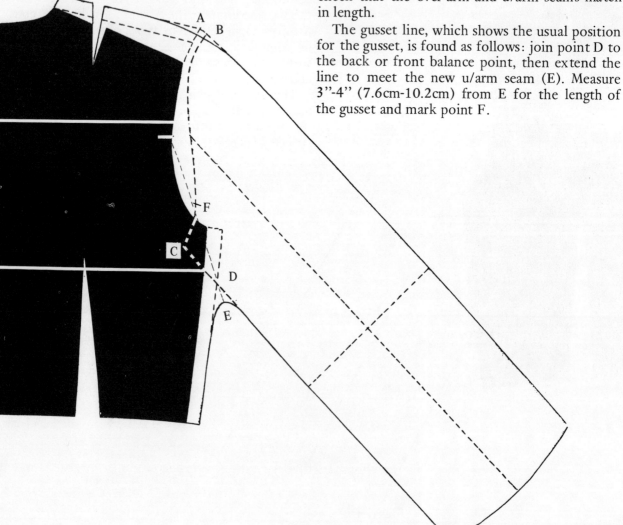

Gussets

The usual position for a gusset is found as described on the previous page.

The longer the gusset, the wider it may be and although in theory a gusset should replace all the lost u/arm length, this is not usually possible as the gusset would need to be very wide.

A gusset should be cut on the bias whenever possible as this gives additional stretch and thus ease of movement.

Types of gusset are:

standard diamond-shaped gusset (shown below)
strip gusset (page 140)
shortened strip gusset (page 141)
gusset incorporated in a yoke−1 (page 142)
gusset incorporated in a yoke−2 (page 143)
gusset incorporated in a panel seam (page 144)

Diamond shaped gusset

This is the most commonly used as it is the least conspicuous.

Outline the back kimono block and draw the gusset line. Mark the gusset point (A) 3½" (8.9cm) from the u/arm point (B).

Measure ½" (13mm) each side of B (C and D) and curve from C and D to A. Cut along the line C-A-D and cut along the gusset line to within $\frac{1}{8}$" (3mm) of A. Spread the sections apart approximately 3" (7.6cm) and correct the curve of the lower edge, as shown. The gusset will be most successful if it is cut on the bias.

Adapt the front kimono block in the same way and, if desired, the gwo gussets may be joined along the line C-D thus forming a diamond shape. There will be a small gap at the centre when they are joined.

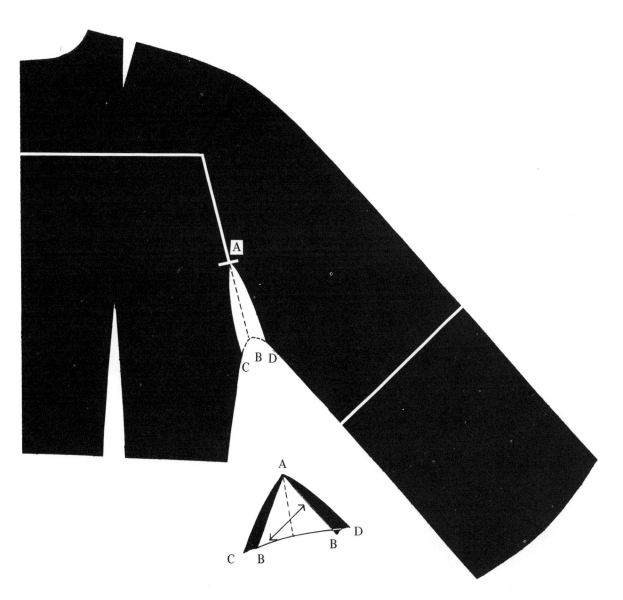

Strip gusset

This type of gusset is frequently used as it is relatively inconspicuous, easy to set-in and replaces almost all of the lost u/arm length, thus fitting closely under the arm. The strip may be made very narrow, e.g. 1"-1½" (2.5cm-3.8cm) so that it is as inconspicuous as possible or it may be wider and incorporated into a seam which is part of the design of the garment. The wider the strip, the more length it will replace. The strip may extend from wrist to hem or it may be shortened, as shown on the following page.

Outline the back kimono block.

Draw a line parallel to the u/arm seam 1"-2" (2.5cm-5.0cm) from it, from waist to wrist. Cut the strip away and cut it along the gusset line from u/arm point (A) almost to the top edge (B). Make two more cuts each side of A, ½" (13mm) apart. Open out the strip until it is *almost* a straight line—it is advisable to leave a slight curve around the gusset line as the strip is then wider at that point to allow extra ease under the arm. Correct the curve of the top edge of the strip and draw the lower edge as a straight line, as shown. The front pattern may then be cut in the same way and the two strips joined along their straight edges. A better fit is obtained by cutting the strip on the bias.

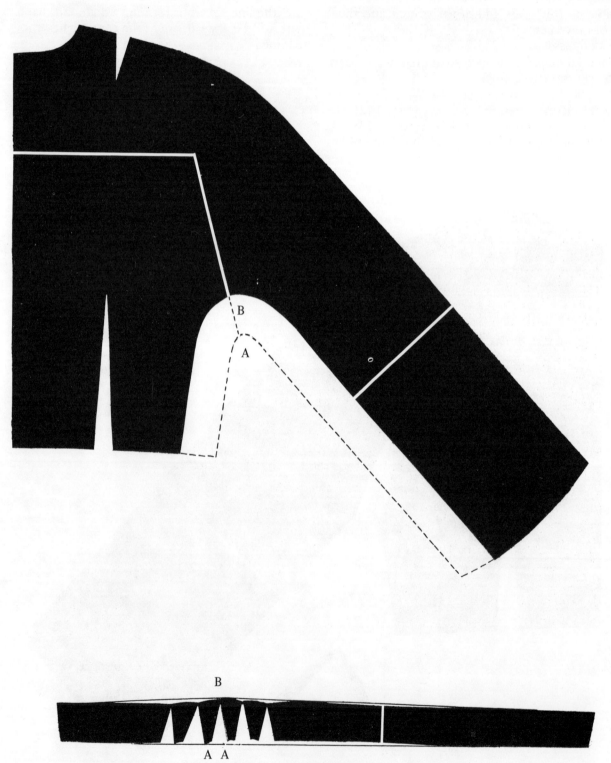

Shortened strip gusset

This gusset has all the advantages of the long strip gusset shown on the previous page, except that it is slightly more difficult to set in, but with the added advantage that it is less conspicuous as it does not extend to the waist or wrist.

Outline the back kimono block.

Measure 3'' (7.6cm) from the u/arm point (A) in each direction (B and C). Draw a line parallel to the u/arm seam 1''-2'' (2.5cm-5.0cm) from it and curve the line into B and C as shown. (This avoids having to set in any corners which are likely to tear.) Cut the strip away and cut from A along the gusset line to within $\frac{1}{8}$'' (3mm) of the top edge. Make three more cuts each side of A, ½'' (13mm) apart. Spread the sections apart until the lower edge is a straight line as shown.

The front pattern may be cut in the same way and the two strips joined along their straight edges so that they may be cut in one piece. Cut the strip on the bias if possible.

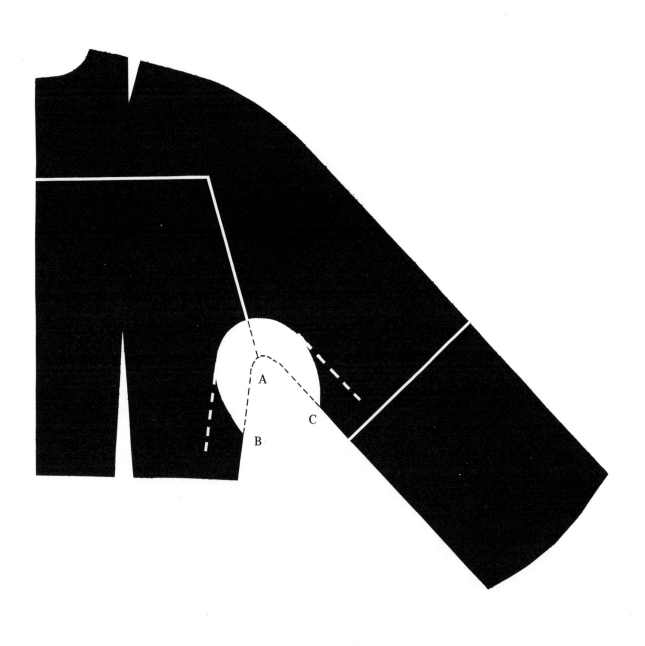

Gusset incorporated in a yoke—1

A gusset incorporated in a yoke or panel seam is completely invisible since it forms part of the design of the garment.

Outline the back kimono block. (The diagram shows the block as far as the elbow line only, to save space.)

Draw the yoke line in the required position (usually following the back width line and the back arm line and curving across the gusset line, as shown). Make balance marks.

Cut along the yoke line, then cut along the gusset line in the lower part to within $\frac{1}{8}$" (3mm) of the yoke seam (point A). Spread the sections apart 2"-3" (7.6cm-10.2cm) at the u/arm point (B). Correct the curves of yoke seam and u/arm seam.

Make the front pattern in the same way.

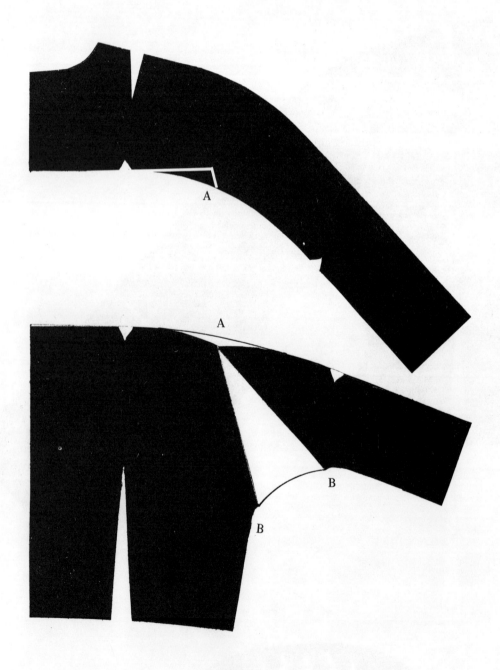

Gusset incorporated in a yoke—2

Outline the back kimono block. Draw the yoke line in the required position (the diagram shows the yoke drawn along the back width line and the gusset line extended to meet the back width line at A).

Cut along the yoke line. On the lower section —measure down ½" (13mm) from the u/arm point (B) to C and join to A. Cut from C to within ⅛" (3mm) of A and snip into the narrow section at intervals. Curve the section around until 2"-3" (5.0cm-7.6cm) has been added at C. The curve thus obtained between A and B gives a better fit than would a straight line.

Correct the curve of the u/arm seam by curving it to B as shown. (The small triangle below B would be cut away.)

Make the front pattern in the same way.

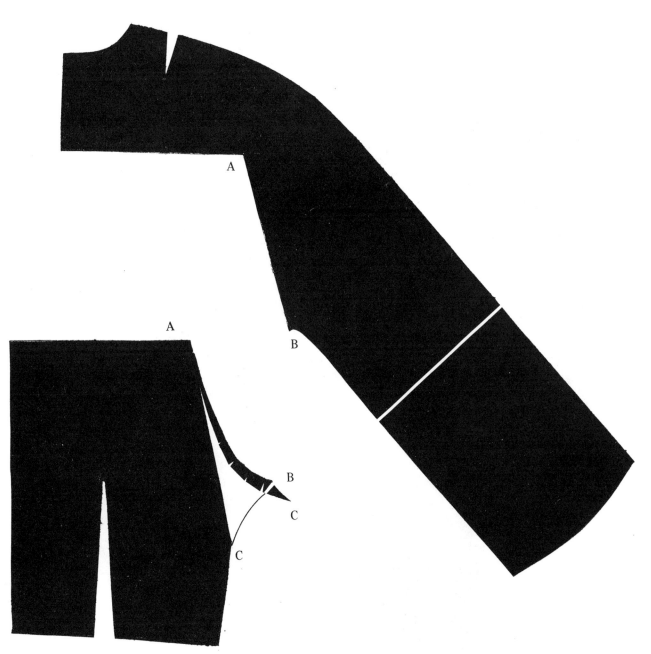

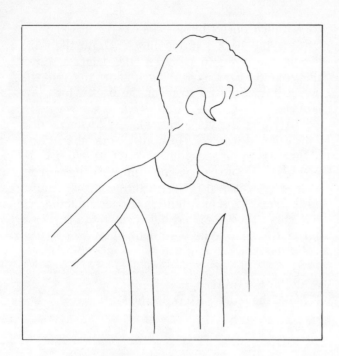

Gusset incorporated in a panel seam

This is not strictly a kimono style as it is cut from the bodice and sleeve blocks, not the kimono block. The lower part of the a/h is set-in, but the upper part has the appearance of a kimono sleeve until the arm is raised.

Bodice

Outline the back bodice block and centralise the shoulder and side seams. Draw the panel seam in the required position (the diagram shows the seam curved from the point of the waist dart (B) to the back width line (A)). Make balance marks as shown and cut the panel away. Smooth the curve of the side panel, which will be slightly pointed at B where the end of the dart occurred. The straight grain line on the side panel should be at right angles to the waist, as shown.

Raise the shoulder point ½" (13mm) (C).

Sleeve

Cut the sleeve block along the centre line. Place the top of the s/h to point C and swing the sleeve until a/h and s/h are touching at point A. (The s/h may overlap the a/h slightly between C and A.) Correct the curve of the overarm seam at the shoulder, by-passing C.

Make the front pattern in the same way.

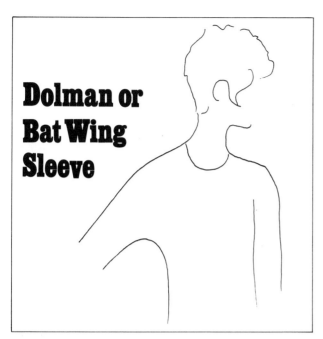

Dolman or Bat Wing Sleeve

Join the u/arm point (A) to the shoulder point (B) and cut from A to within $\frac{1}{8}$" (3mm) of B. Spread the sections apart until the u/arm seam is equal in length to the side seam of the bodice block plus the side seam of the sleeve block. For instance, if the combined bodice and sleeve seams measured 24" (57cm) and the u/arm seam of the kimono block measured 19" (43.5cm) the sections would be spread apart 5" (12.7cm).

Correct the curve of the overarm seam at B and curve the u/arm seam from the waist, by-passing A, to the wrist as shown. The curving of the u/arm seam will reduce the u/arm length again, but because the sleeve is so loose it would still be comfortable to wear.

The dolman sleeve has a very loose, low a/h, often curving as low as the waist. The pattern is made from the kimono block by cutting it along the gusset line and spreading it apart to incorporate most of the u/arm length which was lost when the kimono block was made (see page 136). It therefore does not need a gusset.

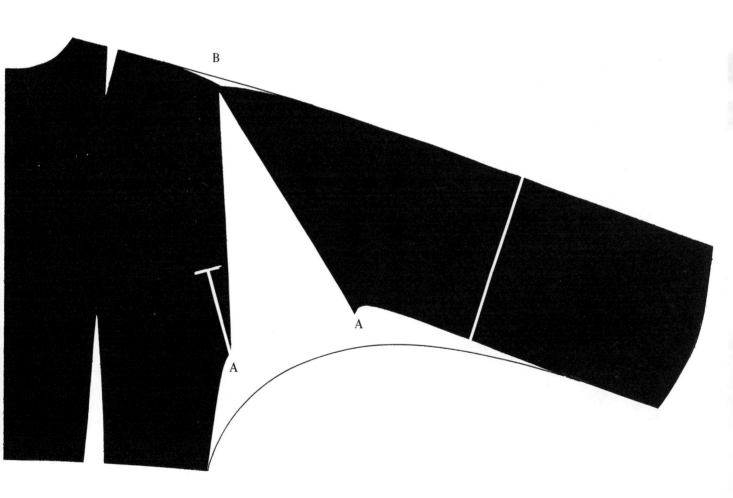

145

Magyar or Cap Sleeve

Bodice
Outline the back bodice block and centralize the shoulder and side seams. Raise the shoulder point ¼" (6mm) (point A) and connect it to the neck point.

Sleeve
Cut the sleeve block along the centre line and place the back sleeve with the top of the s/h at point A. Swing the sleeve until the u/arm point touches the bodice side seam (point B). Outline the sleeve block. Cut along the u/arm line to obtain the hem line; thus the sleeve will measure approximately 6" (15.2cm) from the shoulder point.

This sleeve is normally made without a gusset as the diagram shows that very little u/arm length has been lost.

Make the front pattern in the same way and check that the bodice side seam—from B to the waist—is the same length on back and front.

This is a very short kimono sleeve with no u/arm seam. It is frequently used on summer dresses.

The pattern can most easily be cut from the bodice and sleeve blocks, rather than from the kimono block.

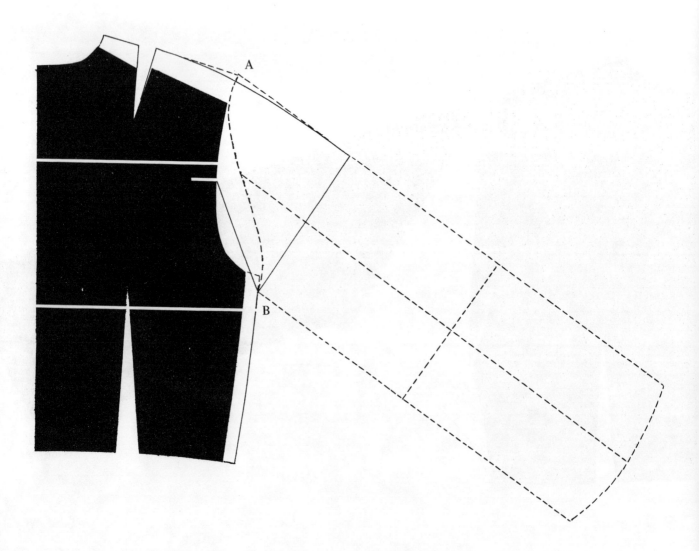

Skirts and Trousers

Skirts

The skirt plays an important part in shaping the silhouette of the figure because of the great variation possible in both length and hem width.

Skirts may vary from very straight, or even tapering inwards at the hem, to very full, with hem width introduced either by gores or circular cutting to give an 'A' shaped silhouette, or by pleats or gathers to give a bell shape. A narrow skirt may have a small amount of fullness at the waist, e.g. gathers or unpressed pleats, but still retain a slim outline.

A gored skirt has four or more vertical seams and is cut to flare at each of the seams. The outline may be varied by changing the positions of seams, the amount of flare added to each seam and the level at which the flare begins. A gored skirt may also be gathered or pleated at the waist to give extra hem width.

Pleated skirts may have all-round knife, box or accordian pleats, single pleats at c/f, c/b or side, or spaced pleats such as the two inverted pleats shown on page 164.

Four Gore Skirt Block

This adaptation from the basic skirt block is also called a block because further styles are adapted from it.

The skirt is divided into four panels by seams at the c/f, c/b and sides, and it flares from just above the hip line. The waist darts are not visible, having been moved into the seams.

Outline the back skirt block (Diag 1)

Add 1" (2.5cm) extra flare at the side seam (A) joining to the original seam just above the hip line, and add 1" (2.5cm) at the centre back (B), joining to the waistline. Extend the centre line of the dart to the hem (C) (diag 1). Cut from C to within $\frac{1}{8}$" (3mm) of the point of the dart and spread the two sections apart at the hem until the sides of the dart meet (diag 2). Outline the pattern on a new sheet of paper. Draw the straight grain line by joining the centre point of the waistline (D) to the centre point of the hem line (E). (The quickest method is to fold the pattern in half lengthways.) The hip line is now slightly curved.

Front
Outline the front skirt block.

Add 1" (2.5cm) extra flare to the side seam and centre front, as for the back block. Extend the dart to 5" (10.2cm below the waist (A) (diag 3) and cut out the new dart. Draw a line from A to the hem (B), parallel to the c/f. Cut from B to within $\frac{1}{8}$" (3mm) of A and spread the sections apart at the hem until the sides of the dart meet (diag 4). Outline the pattern on a new sheet of paper and draw the straight grain line and hip line as for the back block.

This adaptation gives a hem width of approx 60" (142cm) in a 36" (91.5cm) hip size and 20" (51cm) length. If more fullness is required the block must be cut and spread apart as shown on pages 155 and 156.

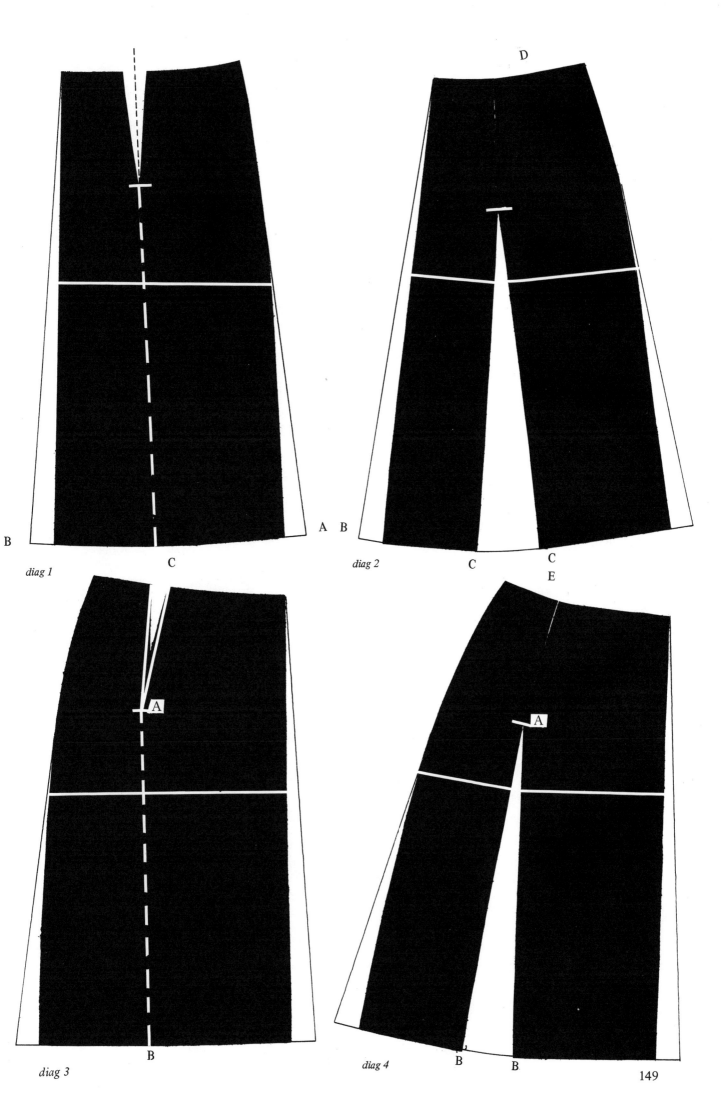

B

C

diag 1

A B

C

C

D

diag 2

E

A

B

diag 3

A

B B

diag 4

149

Four Panelled Skirt

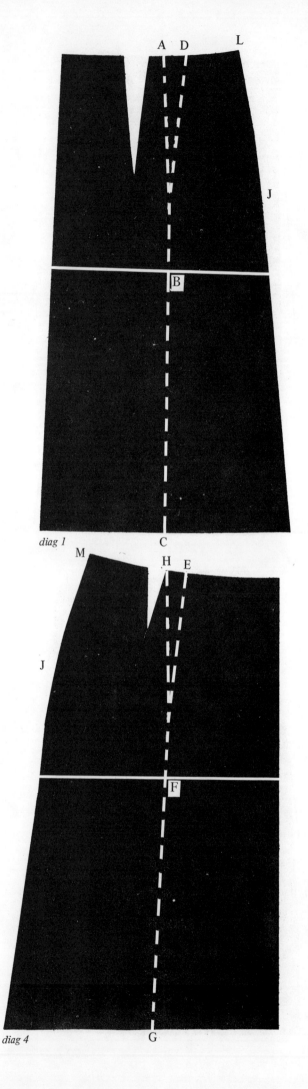

diag 1

diag 4

This skirt is similar to that shown on the previous page in that it is also cut in four panels, but the seams are differently positioned. There are no c/f, c/b or side seams but two side front seams, as shown in the sketch, and two side back seams.

Outline the back skirt block and centralize the side seam. Add 1" (2.5 cm) extra flare to the side seam. Alternatively, the back four-gore block may be outlined, with the c/b vertical.

Mark the centre point of the waist line (A) (disregarding the dart), the centre point of the hip line (B), and the centre point of the hem line (C) (diag 1). Join C-B and continue the line towards the waist for several inches. Curve to A. From A measure the width of the waist dart towards the side seam (D). Curve from just above B to D. Cut along C-B-A and B-D to separate the two panels, as shown in diags 2 and 3. Disregard the dart shown in diagram 2 as it has now been transferred into the seam.

Adapt the front pattern in the same way (diag 4) and cut along the panel line to separate the sections as shown in diagrams 5 and 6. The side panels, diagrams 3 and 5, are now joined along the lower part of the side seam (J-K) with the curves at the top of each side seam forming a dart (L-M). Diags 2, 3 and 5 and 6 show the finished pattern.

The straight grain on the centre front and centre back panels is parallel to the centre lines, as they will be placed to folds when cutting out, and the straight grain of the side panel is parallel to the original side seam, J-K.

The skirt may be made more flared by adding equal amounts (not more than 1" (2.5 cm) at points C and G.

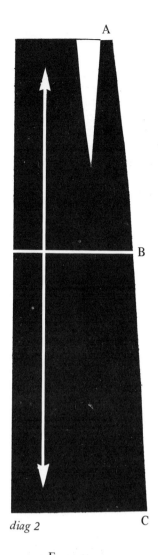

diag 2

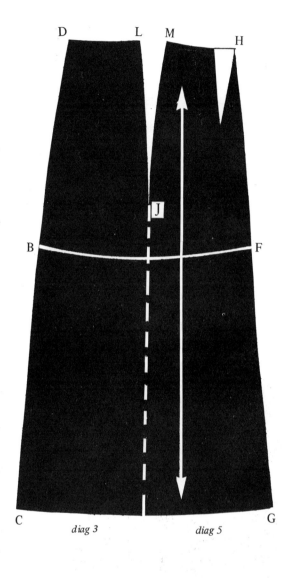

diag 3   *diag 5*

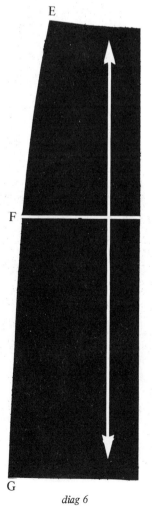

diag 6

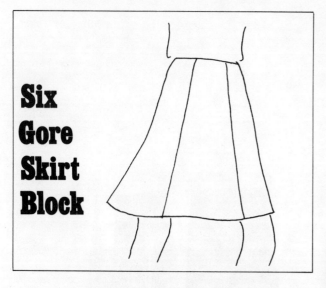

Six Gore Skirt Block

Cut along the line C-D-E (diag 2). The straight grain line of the side panel may be found by folding the pattern in half lengthways, as for the four-gore block, and the straight grain line of the centre panel is parallel to the c/b line.

Make the front patterns in the same way.

The hem width will be the same as that of the four-gore skirt, although more fullness may be added by cutting through the centre of each panel and spreading it apart, as shown on the following page and on page 155.

Outline the back four-gore block (page 148) with the c/b vertical. Centralise the side seam (to ensure that all the six panels are equal in width.)

Measure the hem line (A-B). From A, measure one-third of A-B towards B (C). Repeat the procedure at the hip line to find D and at the waist line to find E. Join C-D with a straight line and join D-E with a slight curve if necessary (diag 1).

(N.B. The side panel must be twice the width of the centre panel because the centre back line will be placed to a fold of fabric and thus the panel will be doubled in width.)

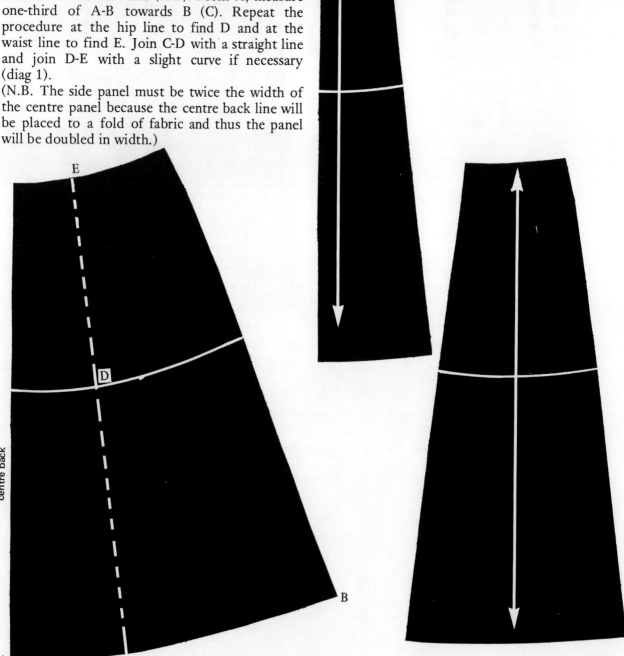

Trumpet Skirt

Adapt the four-gore block to a six-gore skirt as shown on the previous page.

Draw a curve parallel to the hip line at the level at which the flare is required to begin (A-B) on each of the six pattern pieces. Cut along the line A-B and cut the lower part of the pattern into three equal sections as shown. Spread the sections apart until the required hem width is obtained. (The lower the cut across is made, the less the sections may be spread apart because the angle between the side edges and the straight grain line should not be greater than 30° (the angle shown in the diagram).

Correct the curves of the side edges and hem and draw the straight grain line in the centre of the panel as shown.

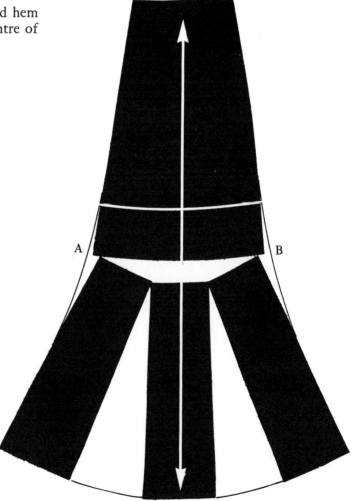

Flared skirts from the Four Gore Block

Outline the back four-gore skirt block and centralize the side seam. The side seam must also be straightened by adding 1½" (3.8cm) at the hem (A) and joining it to the waist. Divide the waist line into three equal parts (B and C) and the hem line into three equal parts (D and E) and join corresponding points as shown in diag 1. (The block is prepared in this way for all the adaptations shown in diags 2, 3 and 4.) Cut from D to within $\frac{1}{8}$" (3mm) of B and from E to within $\frac{1}{8}$" of C and spread the sections apart, adding the same amount at each line, to obtain the required hem width (diag 2). Fold the pattern in half lengthways to find the straight grain line.

Make the front pattern in the same way.

Circular skirt (diag 3)
Outline the back four-gore skirt block and adapt it as shown in diag 1.

Cut along the lines D-B and E-C almost to the waist and spread the sections apart until the side seam is at right angles to the c/b. Make the front pattern in the same way. The c/b and c/f may each be placed to a fold when cutting out so that the skirt has two seams at the sides, or the front and back patterns may be joined at the side and the skirt cut with one seam, at the c/b, which must be on the straight grain.

Semi-circular skirt (diag 4)
Outline the back four-gore block and adapt it as shown in diag 1. Cut the pattern along the lines D-B and E-C almost to the waist and spread the sections apart until the side seam is at 45° to the c/b. Like the circular skirt, this skirt may also be cut with a c/b seam only and again the seam must be on the straight grain. The c/f will also be on the straight grain and the side seams on the bias.

Because the pattern is cut from the hem to the waist in all these adaptations, the skirt will begin to flare from the waist, not the hip line as is the

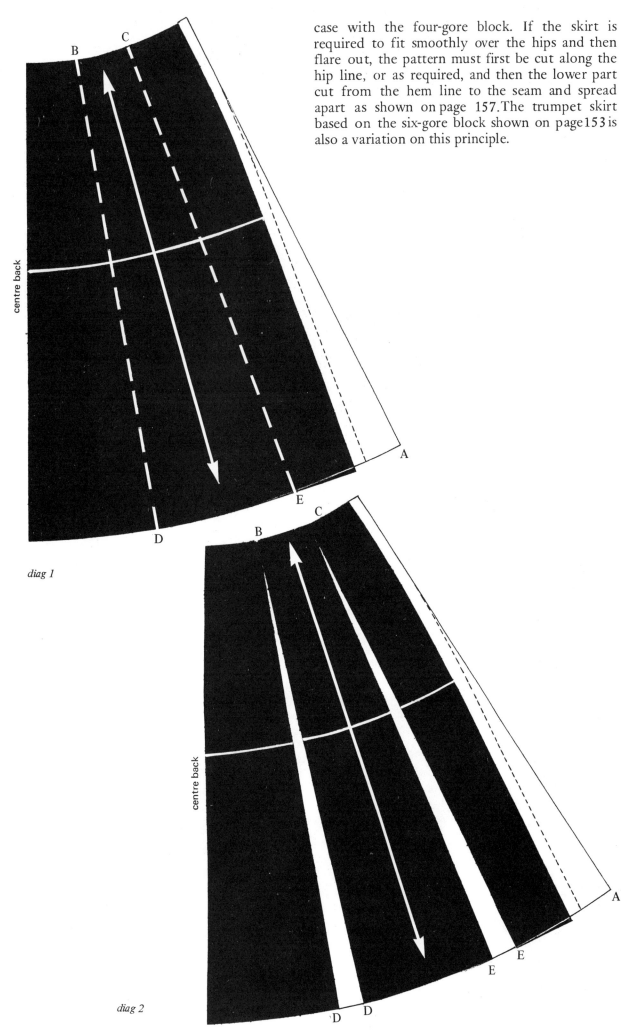

case with the four-gore block. If the skirt is required to fit smoothly over the hips and then flare out, the pattern must first be cut along the hip line, or as required, and then the lower part cut from the hem line to the seam and spread apart as shown on page 157. The trumpet skirt based on the six-gore block shown on page 153 is also a variation on this principle.

centre back

B

C

A

E

D

diag 1

centre back

C

B

A

E

E

E

D

D

diag 2

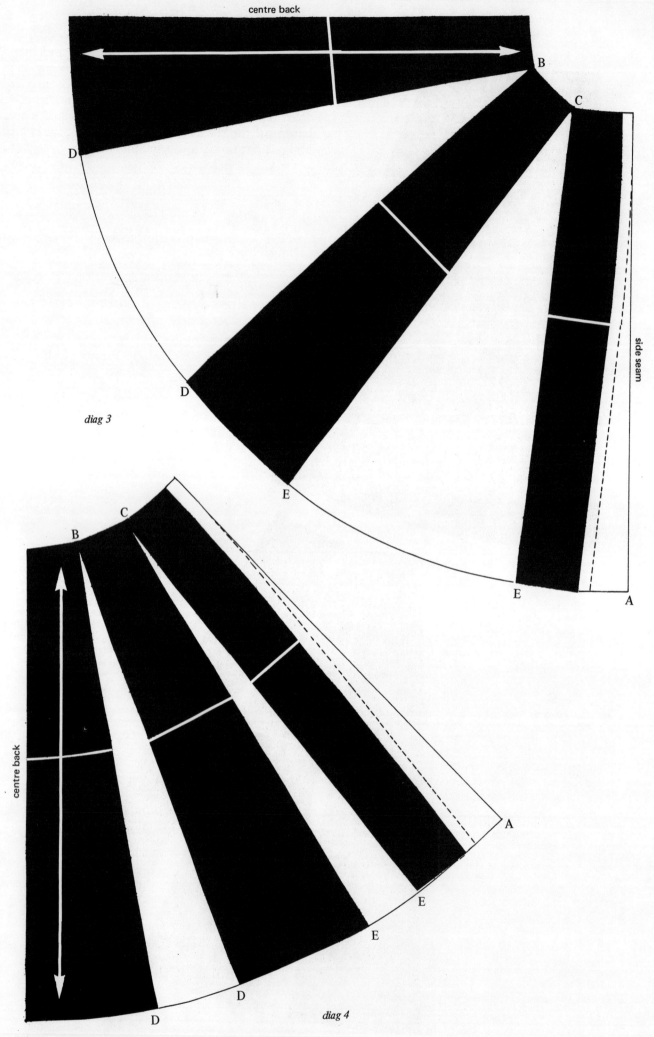

centre back

B

C

side seam

D

D

E

A

diag 3

C

B

centre back

A

E

E

D

D

diag 4

156

Circular Skirt with Yoke

This adaptation enables the skirt to be very wide at the hem while fitting closely over the hips.

Outline the back four-gore block and centralize and straighten the side seam (see diag 1, page 155). Draw the yoke line in the required position (A-B). Make balance marks as shown and cut along the line A-B. Divide the hem line into three (C and D) and the line A-B into three (E and F) and join corresponding points. Cut along each line from the hem to within $\frac{1}{8}$'' (3mm) of E and F and spread the sections apart until the side seam is at right angles to the c/b.

Correct the curves of the top edge and hem.

Make the front pattern in the same way.

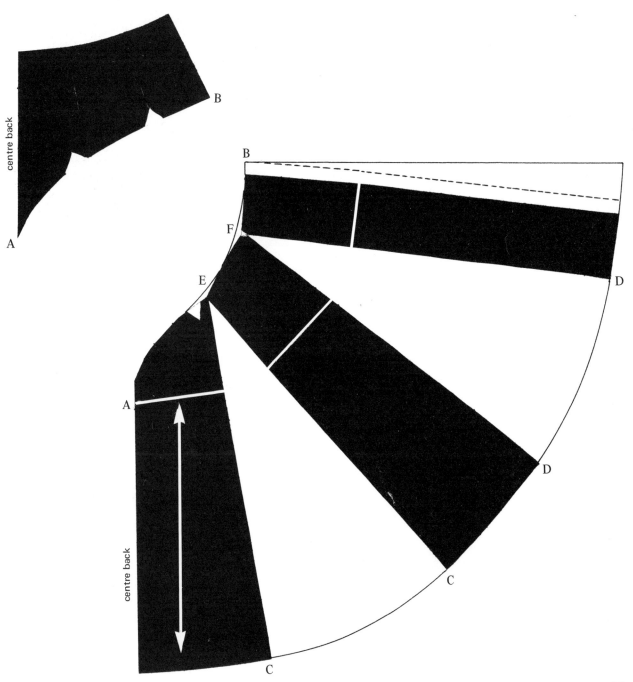

Godets

Godets are triangular-shaped inserts used to give extra width at the hem while keeping the top of the skirt close-fitting. They may be inserted into a seam or into a slit cut in the fabric. A skirt with godets has a very similar silhouette to the trumpet skirt (page 153), i.e. fitting smoothly to below the hip line and then flaring suddenly.

Outline the back skirt block or four-gore block as required. If using the basic skirt block (as shown in the diagram) add 1" (2.5cm) extra flare to the side seam. Mark a point one-third of the hem width from the c/b (A) and draw a line from A to the hip line parallel to the c/b. Mark the length of godet required (B).

Draw a triangle C-D-E in which C-D and C-E are equal to A-B on the skirt pattern and D-E measures the required hem width of the godet, which should be slightly less than its length. Curve the line D-E as shown. The straight grain line is parallel to the centre line of the triangle.

Godets may also be set into the seams of the six-gore skirt (page 152).

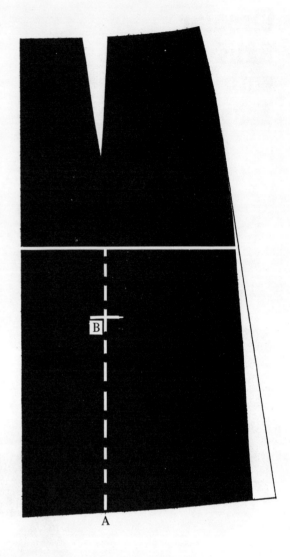

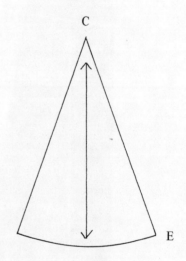

Wrapover Skirt

A wrapover skirt must have sufficient overlap to prevent it gaping and needs considerably more fabric than would at first be assumed.

Back (diag 1)
Outline the back skirt block and add 1" (2.5cm) extra flare at the side seam. Also cut through the block to the point of the dart and add 1" (2.5cm) flare at the hem. (The dart will then be reduced to approximately ½" (13mm).

Right front (diag 2)
Outline the front skirt block, allowing approximately 12" (30.5cm) margin beyond the c/f, and add 1" extra flare at the side seam and at the centre by cutting through the pattern to the point of the dart, as for the back. (There is no need to re-draw the pattern after adding the 1" (2.5cm) at the centre—a strip of paper may be stuck beneath the slit.)

Fold the pattern along the c/f line and trace the waist and hemline curves on the margin allowed. Decide on the position of the wrap line—usually approximately 5" (12.7cm) beyond the c/f. Measure 5" (12.7cm) (or as required) from the c/f and draw a parallel line (A-B). The wrapover will hang best if this line is on the straight grain, which also enables the wrap facing to be cut in one piece with the skirt. The facing should be at least 1"-2" (2.5cm-5.0cm) wider than the overlap so that it extends to beyond the c/f. Add 7" (17.8cm) (or as required) to the wrap line (A-B) and draw a parallel line (C-D). Fold the pattern along A-B and trace the waist and hemline curves on to the facing.

Left front (diag 3)
Outline the complete front skirt block as shown in diag 3. Add 1" (2.5cm) to the side seam and to the centre of the block by cutting through, as for the right front. Only the part of the pattern to the right of the wrap line will be visible when the skirt is made up—the remainder forms the under

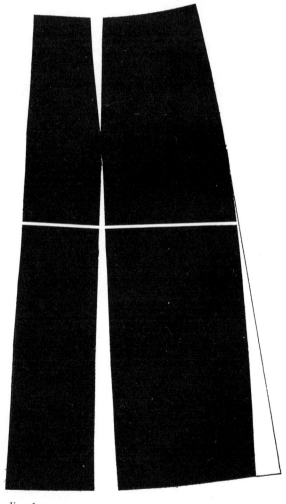

diag 1

part of the wrap and should extend to approximately 1" (2.5cm) from the side seam to ensure that the skirt does not gape (E-F). The edge of the under part (E-F) is cut off-grain to increase the width of the overlap at the hem without causing bulk at the waist, and it would need to be strengthened with tape to prevent it dropping.

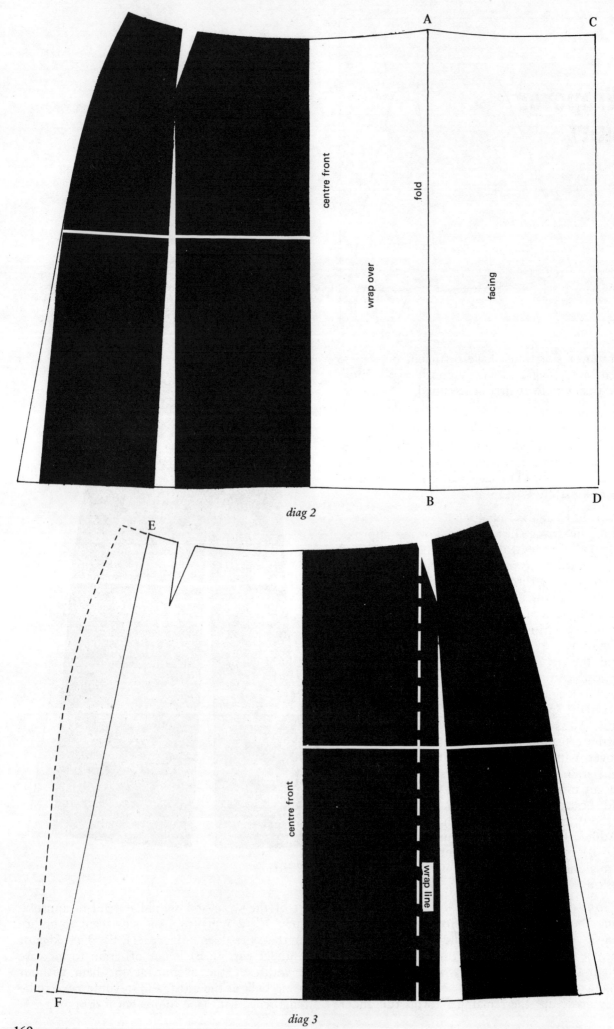

diag 2

diag 3

Pleated Skirts

Continuous (i.e. all-round) pleated skirts give fullness, freedom of movement and vertical interest, although the silhouette is only slightly flared. Unpressed pleats create a silhouette similar to that of a gathered skirt, i.e. a bell shape. The average hem width for a pleated skirt is three times the hip m/ment (the minimum is twice the hip m/ment otherwise the skirt will appear skimpy). A pattern is often not needed because, before pleating, the skirt will simply be a rectangle measuring the length required, by hip m/ment x 3, plus seam and hem allowances. The pleats must be calculated to fit exactly into the hip m/ment, e.g. for a 36" (91.5cm) hip m/ment the skirt should measure 39" (99cm) (1" (2.5cm) extra ease to compensate for the extra layers of fabric) and thus 39 1" (2.5cm) or 26 1½" (3.8cm) pleats could be used. The pleats are overlapped above the hip line to reduce the top of the skirt to the required waist m/ment. The fold of each pleat should be on the straight grain to enable the pleats to hang well, except for accordian pleating. Pleats should not be made in bulky material.

Straight pleats (i.e. those in which the outer and inner folds are on the straight grain)
These are always used for all-round pleated skirts and may be used for very short pleats, e.g. at the c/b of a narrow skirt, but otherwise shaped pleats are usually more successful.

Shaped pleats
Shaped pleats are wider at the hem than at the top edge. They hang better than straight pleats and are less likely to open at the hem, but the inner edges must be handled carefully and taped to prevent them stretching.

If pleats hang badly it may be because of one of these reasons:
The skirt is too narrow at the hem
The pleats are too narrow
The pleats have been cut off-grain or the edges stretched during pressing
The seams or the hem inside the pleat may be badly sewn or pressed
The pleat may be insufficiently supported.

Short inverted pleat
A short pleat in the c/b seam of a narrow skirt increases the hem width to allow for easier movement while retaining the narrow outline.
Outline the back skirt block.

Decide on the finished width of the pleat (usually 5"-6" (12.7cm-15.2cm)) and add half that amount (A) plus ½" (13mm) (B) to the c/b hemline. (The extra ½" (13mm) is added to avoid the join between pleat extension and underlay being on the inside edge of the pleat, thus creating problems when the hem is turned up.) Square up from B for the length of pleat required (C), which is usually 6"-7" (15.2cm-17.8cm) and square across to the c/b (D) to complete the pleat extension.

The pleat underlay (diag 2) is therefore cut 1" (2.5cm) narrower than the desired finished width of the pleat to compensate for the ½" (13mm) added to the block. The top corners of the pleat must always be supported by tapes sewn into the c/b seam.

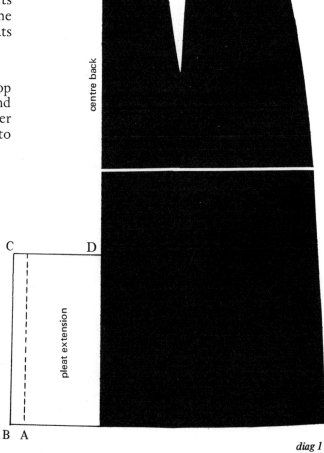

diag 1

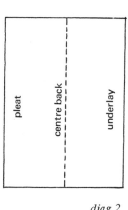

diag 2

161

Centre front inverted pleat
This pattern has a full length shaped pleat, i.e. the pleat extends to the waist, but the pleat edges would probably be sewn down for 5"-6" (12.7cm-15.2cm) below the waist.

Outline the front skirt block and add 1" (2.5cm) extra flare at the side seam. On the c/f line add 2" (5.0cm) at the waist (A) and 4" (10.2cm) at the hem (B) (or required amounts) for the pleat extension and join A-B. Fold the pleat extension under along the c/f line and trace the shape of waist and hem curves.

Make the width of the pleat underlay (diag 2) twice the amount added to the skirt block—4" (10.2cm) at the waist and 8" (20.3cm) at the hem—with the straight grain line parallel to the centre line and waist and hem lines curved to match the pleat extension.

(Although it is possible to avoid having seams along the inside edges of a straight pleat (see page 161) it cannot be avoided in a shaped pleat as the method used on page 161 would result in the inside edges being off-grain and they would therefore stretch easily and drop.)

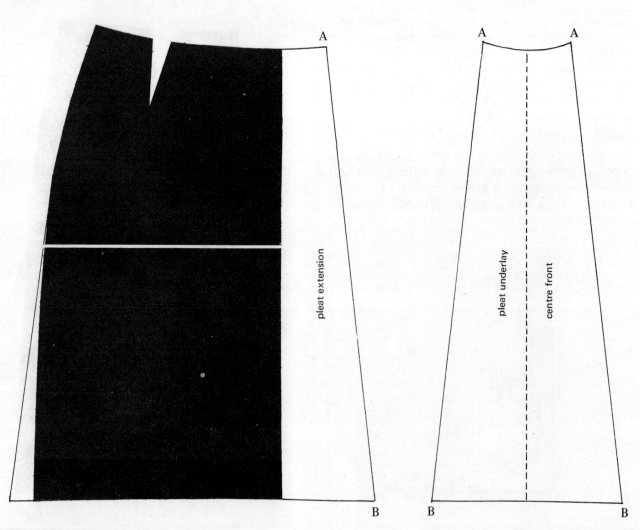

Centre front inverted pleat with yoke

A yoke seam is a very successful means of supporting the pleat edges so that they hang attractively. Outline the front skirt block and add 1" (2.5cm) extra flare at the side seam.

Draw the yoke line in the required position, make balance marks and cut along it. Extend the dart to the yoke line if necessary and fold out the dart, as shown. Proceed as for the full length pleat on the previous page. It is especially important that the pleat extension is folded under and the shape of the top edge traced, as otherwise the pleat edges may not be supported in the yoke seam.

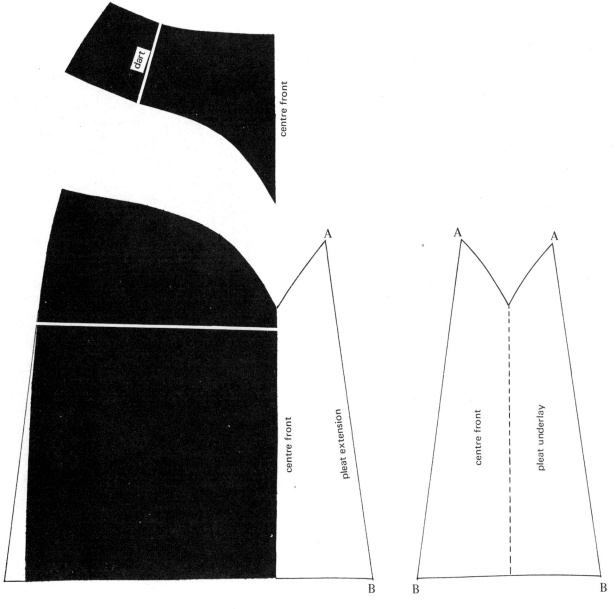

Pleated Skirts

Spaced pleats

Spaced pleats are those which do not extend all round the skirt. Like the single inverted pleat on the previous page, the pleats are set into a yoke as this is the most successful way of supporting the pleats.

Outline the front skirt block and add 1'' (2.5cm) extra flare at the side seam. Draw the yoke line in the required position, curved or pointed, and draw the positions of the pleats (diag 1).

Make balance marks and cut along the yoke line, extend the dart to the edge of the yoke and fold out the dart. The pleats shown here are shaped pleats, i.e. wider at the hem than the top. Decide on the required depth of the pleat at hem and top edge and draw the pleat extensions and underlays as shown, equal in width. (The pleat extension is the section which folds back.)

Fold the pattern along the pleat lines and place the three sections together as they will be when made up. Cut along the curve of the top edge through all thicknesses. Draw the straight grain line on each section parallel to the pleat edges.

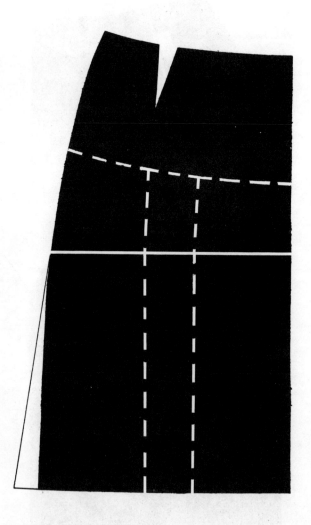

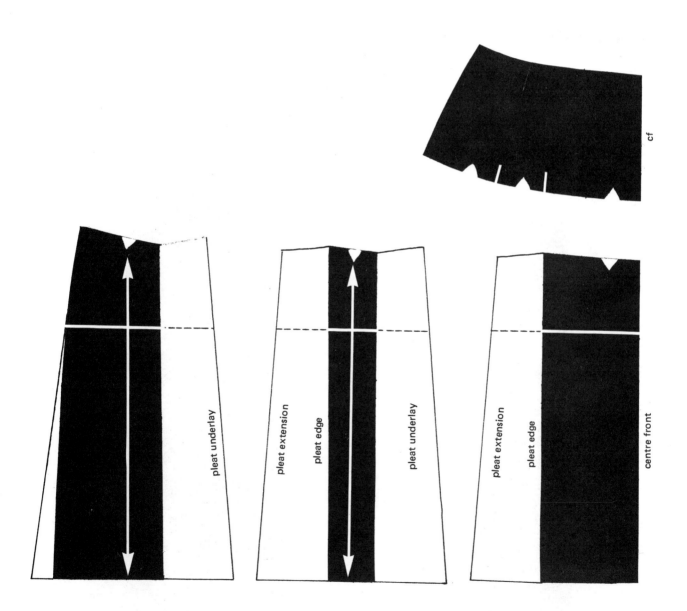

Built-up Waistline

This adaptation is likely to be most successful if it is made in conjunction with the six-gore skirt pattern.

Decide on the required depth of the extension above the waist. Measure the figure at that level and add 1" (2.5cm) for ease. Divide that m/ment by six, i.e. a figure m/ment of 29" (72.5cm), plus 1" (2.5cm) ease equals 30" (75cm); therefore each panel must measure 5" (10.2cm) along the top edge.

Outline the back section of the six-gore block. Draw a curve parallel to the waist line 3" (7.6cm) above it at (A-B), or as required. Continue the c/b line upwards and measure 2½" (6.3cm) (i.e. half of 5" (10.2cm)) from the c/b along the line A-B. Curve from B into the skirt seam.

Outline the side back section of the six-gore block. Draw a curve parallel to the waistline, 3" (7.6cm) above it at (C-D) and continue the centre line upwards. Measure 2½" (6.3cm) each side of the centre line on the line C-D and curve into the skirt seams, slightly bypassing the waist if necessary to give a good curve.

Make the front patterns in the same way.

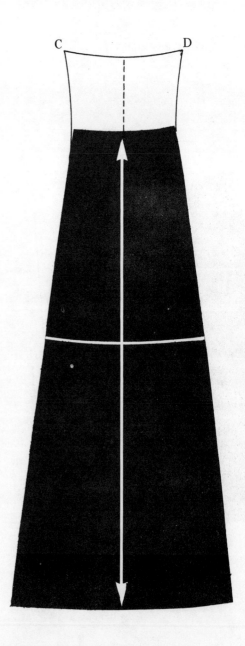

Cullotte Skirt

The culotte skirt is a skirt with a crotch section added to allow freedom of movement. It usually has an inverted pleat at the c/f and c/b to give it the appearance of a skirt, such as that on page   .
Without the pleat, the culotte skirt would have the appearance of very loose-fitting shorts. It has a lower crotch line than the trouser block to give additional ease of movement. The culotte skirt is often used for sportswear, particularly tennis dresses.

Front
Outline the front skirt block (diag 1). Add 1"
(2.5cm) extra flare at the c/f (A) and join to the waist (B). The line A-B then becomes the c/f line and the straight grain line is drawn parallel to it. 1" (2.5cm) may also be added to the side seam.
Measure the crotch depth plus 1" (2.5cm) down

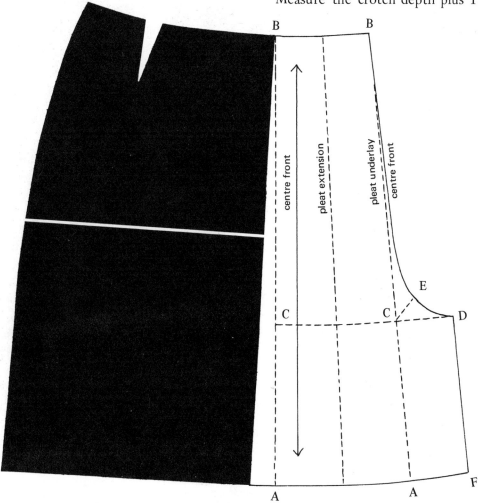

from B and mark point C. Add the required
amounts at A and B for the pleat, which should
preferably be a shaped pleat (see page 162) and
draw the new c/f line (A-C-B). (The diagram
shows 2" (5.0cm) added at the waist and 3"
(7.6cm) at the hem.) Fold the pleat under, as it
will be when sewn, and trace the curve of the
waistline. With the pleat still folded under, square
out from C one-twelfth of hip m/ment less ½"
(13mm) (D). Measure half of C-D from C at 45°
to C-D (E). Curve the c/f seam D-E-B. Square
down from D the same distance as C-A (F) and
curve the hemline.

Back

Outline the back skirt block (diag 2). Add 1"
(2.5cm) extra flare at the c/b (A) and join to the
waist (B). The line A-B now becomes the c/b line
and the straight grain line is drawn parallel to it.
1" (2.5cm) may also be added to the side seam.
Measure the crotch depth plus 1" (2.5cm) down
from B, as for the front pattern, and mark point
C. Raise the c/b waistline ½" (13mm) and curve
to the side waist. Add the same amounts as on the
front pattern for the pleat, and fold the pleat
under. From C, with the pleat folded under,
measure out one-twelfth of hip m/ment (D), and
measure half of C-D plus ½" (13mm) from C at
45° to C-D, (E). Curve the c/b seam D-E-B.
Square down from D to F the same distance as
D-F on the front pattern and curve the hemline.

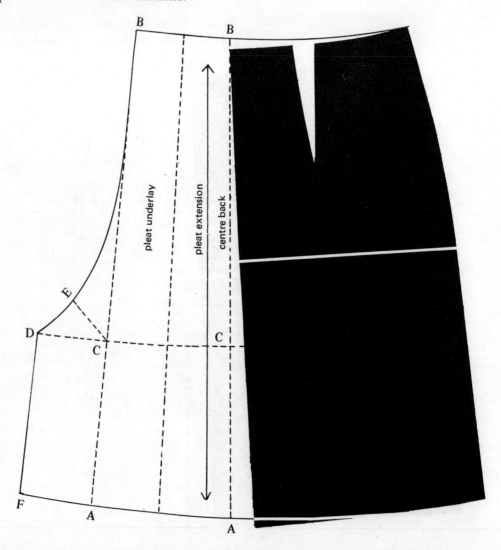

Trousers

Flared trousers
Close-fitting trousers
Shorts

Flared

The trouser block may be widened at the knee line and the hemline, or at the hemline only, according to the shape required. The diagram shows both types of adaptation. The same amount is added to inside and outside leg seams on back and front.

Trousers flared from the crotch line
(solid line in diagram)
Outline the front trouser block. Decide on the required width at the knee and measure one-quarter of that amount each side of the crease line at knee level (A and B). Decide on the hem width and repeat the procedure at the hem (C and D). Join C-A and D-B with straight lines, continuing the lines slightly above A and B. Curve the inside leg seam smoothly to the crotch point (E) and curve the outside leg seam smoothly into the original seam just above the crotch line, as shown. Ensure that the m/ments chosen for knee and hem lines give an attractively shaped pattern.
Adapt the back trouser block in the same way.

Trousers flared from the knee
(broken line in diagram)
Outline the front trouser block. Decide on the required hem width and measure one-quarter of that amount each side of the crease line at the hem (C and D). Join C and D to a point approx 3" (7.6cm) below the knee line (F and G) as a guide. Join C-F and D-G with straight lines, then curve smoothly from that line to the knee line as shown. Adapt the back trouser block in the same way.

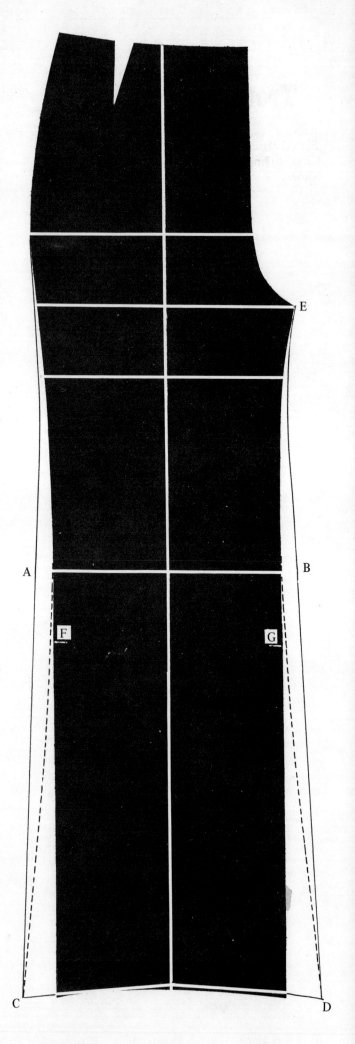

Closefitting Trousers

This pattern should only be made up in stretch fabric as the width at knee and ankle lines has been reduced considerably—to 15" (38cm) and 13" (33cm) respectively.

Outline the front trouser block. Measure 1½" (3.8cm) in at the hemline each side and 1" (2.5cm) at the knee line (or amounts as required). Measure ½" (13mm) in at the crotch point (A). Draw the new side seams and curve the top of the inside leg seam to A. Curve the outside leg seam as shown in the diagram, which reduces the width at the hip line by ¼"-½" (6mm-13mm). Raise the crotch point ¼"-½" (6mm-13mm) as shown.

Adapt the back block in the same way.

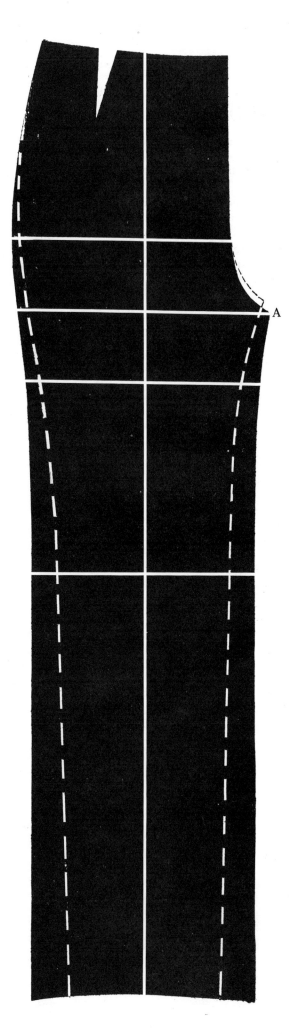

Shorts

Outline the front trouser block. Draw a line across at the length required, parallel to the crotch line (broken line on diag). Curve the line down approx ½" (13mm) at each side to ensure that the hemline is a continuous curve when the shorts are made up. Because the trouser block fits closely at the thigh line, it is not usually necessary to take in the side seams for the shorts pattern.

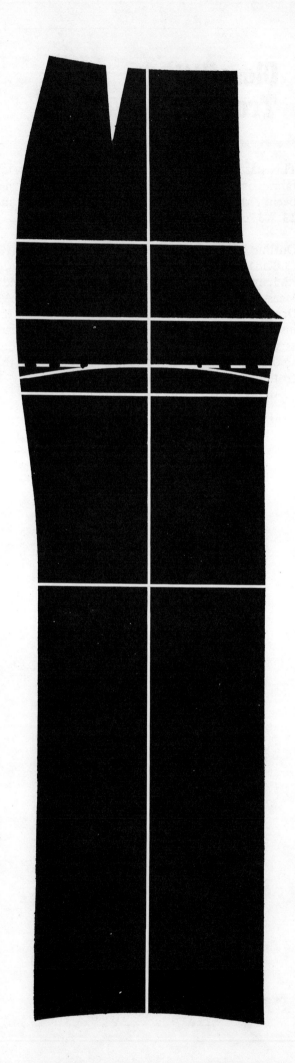